The ADHD
Support Handbook

THE ADHD
SUPPORT HANDBOOK

A real-life guide to
empowering a child with ADHD
and related conditions

Jean Gibson

Rethink

First published in Great Britain in 2021
by Rethink Press (www.rethinkpress.com)

*This book is dedicated to my daughter Lynnette,
a loving, caring person, a wonderful mother and
a supportive daughter*

*To my grandson, Mekhi, an inspirational, loving,
sensitive boy who will no doubt make
a great impact on the world one day*

*To my husband, Frank, a great dad, stepdad and
loving grandad who supports me in all that I do*

*To my parents, whom I loved unconditionally and
to whom I owe everything*

Contents

Foreword

This positive, empowering book is a fantastic resource for families. Jean is a pioneer, passionate about supporting parents with children who struggle to make sense of the world. This book shows that every day is an opportunity to make a difference to our children, to their view of the world and the way they regard themselves. It helps mums, dads and carers to support children in managing a full spectrum of challenging emotions; to put children in the driving seat of their own lives; to give them the tools to climb life's mountain, whatever that looks like; to rise to the challenge and grow stronger.

This is a book for those raising a generation of superheroes. Not the superheroes who wear masks and capes; our children are real superheroes. We can nurture in our little ones the superpowers that will make a difference in our world: compassion, responsibility, empathy, honesty, integrity and love.

Thank you, Jean. This book will make a difference. The world we leave to our children depends on the children we leave in the world.

Lorraine Thomas, Chief Executive, The Parent Coaching Academy (www.theparentcoachingacademy. com), and author of *Super Coach Arty vs The Shadow, Brilliantly Behaved Toddler, The 7-Day Parent Coach, Get A Life* and *The Mummy Coach*

Introduction

In 2018, my grandson, Mekhi, was seven years old and had been diagnosed with attention deficit hyperactivity disorder (ADHD), dyspraxia and developmental delay. The first indication that he had any learning difficulties had been his speech; he received speech therapy, which helped his verbal communication. My daughter and I spent much time discussing his challenges at nursery, and later at school; his excessive tiredness; how difficult it was to get him ready in the morning; his forgetfulness; how he was always losing things; how he never listened or did the things he was asked to do or that were appropriate for his age, like getting himself dressed. At the same time, he was loving, sensitive, highly impulsive and active. We loved his energy. He had great fun playing with Grandad Frankie especially, who let him climb all over him and had the time and energy to play rough and tumble.

Yet I had not taken the time to consider and understand what the conditions Mekhi was dealing with meant to him and our family. It wasn't until June 2019 that I began to understand the impact his energetic behaviour was having. My daughter shared with me her struggle to get the right support for Mekhi at school and confessed that her social circle had disappeared to the point that she had no one to talk to but me. My heart broke for her. As her mother, I felt helpless and overwhelmed by what she was telling me, the lonely journey she was on. What could I do to help her? I decided to start a support group for parents of children with ADHD, autism and other related conditions.

Fast forward to October 2019 and I was doubting my ability to run and add value to the group that I had established. While the first meeting had had three attendees, just one person had attended the last, and they hadn't even been a parent.

I had been quite anxious as I considered how the support group had been received. There had been a lot of interest online and the people I talked to sounded keen, but the meetings weren't well attended, and I began to feel that I was not reaching the right people. This was, in fact, not the case. When I looked more in-depth at the impact the meetings had for those who did attend, I saw that it was exactly the impact I had envisioned and was what the attendees needed. At the first meeting, the two parents who attended had cried with relief while sharing their challenges and learning that they were not alone. My daughter, the third attendee, was similarly emotional at finding others who understood and related to what she was going through and did not judge her. At the second meeting, a man ran up the stairs to the hall and exclaimed, 'I have just seen your poster. I have been diagnosed with ADHD.' He sat with us and felt comfortable enough to share his diagnosis and journey thus far. He was able to learn more about the condition and share his initial thoughts in a safe place. He expressed feeling relieved and vowed to help us grow our numbers, which he did. Even so, I still felt anxious that I was not doing enough.

Sometimes it takes someone who is not close to you to remind you of the impact of what you are doing is having on people's lives. Talking through my concerns and reflecting with my mindset coach, helped me to see that the group was doing exactly what it needed to. I was reminded of why I had wanted to create the group: for the sake of love.

My reason for setting up the support group had been to give my daughter a voice and a community of people she could turn to for support who understood what she was going through, and for us to provide that same support to others; to help other parents feeling the same as Lynnette was and who were going through the same challenges. To give parents and carers the opportunity to verbalise their feelings in a safe, non-judgemental environment so that they no longer felt alone. As a mother and grandmother, I felt the need to let other parents know that there were people they could talk to who would listen and understand without judgement.

The group continues to this day and it is a joy to hear everyone open up about their challenges and successes each month. The laughter is contagious as, on occasion, are the tears as we share our experiences and difficulties and recognise those of others. The non-judgemental support extended in the room is heart-warming. So far, we've had new people attend each month, and their joy at finding a group of people who understand is electric.

The same motivations for creating the support group inspired me to write this book. If you are a parent or carer of a child or children with a developmental disorder such as ADHD, dyspraxia, autism, developmental delay or one of the lesser-known disorders, you may feel alone. You may feel tired, confused, guilty, frustrated and worn out. The constant battle to find information, answers and solutions to help your child can feel never-ending and exhausting. The isolation and judgement from others who don't understand what you are going through can be debilitating.

This book will help you to know that *you are not alone*. A similar story to yours unfolds in many homes, and there is light at the end of the tunnel. You will learn about my struggle with supporting my daughter, Lynnette, through her learning difficulties and find out more about my grandson, Mekhi. Importantly, this book will equip you with a variety of resources, tools, tips and information to help you navigate your journey.

Some resources and links are supplied within the book, and can also be found at https:// activepersonaldevelopment.co.uk/adhd-support-handbook-resources. The password for accessing these resources is ADHDsuccess.

As a life coach, I have used these tools with my clients, as well as with my grandson. I hope you will find them useful.

A common challenge faced by parents and carers is the amount of information they are either given or have to search through to find the materials or guidance they need to move forward. Alongside my tried and tested process of parenting a child with ADHD, as introduced below, I have given you signposts and summarised information that will assist you in your research, regardless of where you are on your journey. The aim is to inspire, educate and empower parents and carers to keep going and know that they are not alone on their journey.

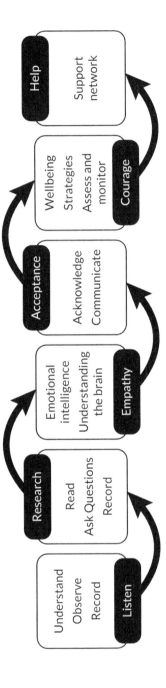

The APD process of parenting a child with ADHD

The APD Process

The Active Personal Development (APD) process of parenting a child with ADHD (which also applies to other similar and related conditions) is based on the key elements that I found were required to support my daughter and grandson, Mekhi. Using this model, he is now getting what he needs to support his development and my daughter is receiving the support she needs to keep going. Each step in the APD process is explored in a chapter in this book and relates to the strengths and characteristics required by parents and carers to successfully support their child.

In my corporate career, I was responsible for creating skills development strategies and competency frameworks for the Information Technology department of a national airline, consisting of over 1,000 people. Drawing on my professional skills and experience, I formulated the APD process as a guide to the different stages you will go through with a child with ADHD or related condition. My aim is that, after reading this book, you will feel empowered and understand the information and skills you will need to support your child.

Each of the following chapters covers one of the six elements of the ADP process. Each element in the process is a pillar supported by other skills or capabilities. Combined, they will support you in your journey. The APD process was developed from lessons learned from my recent and past experiences. Regardless of the condition, diagnosis or situation you are facing, you can use this book as a guide to get the support you need. This book is not about coaching, it is about our journey and how our journey can help you. It's personal!

1
Actively Listen

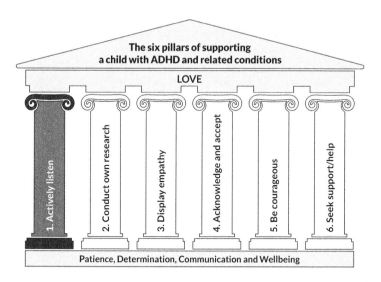

The six pillars of supporting
a child with ADHD and related conditions

LOVE

1. Actively listen

2. Conduct own research

3. Display empathy

4. Acknowledge and accept

5. Be courageous

6. Seek support/help

Patience, Determination, Communication and Wellbeing

I am the second oldest child of four, with an older brother and two younger sisters, all born in the UK. We grew up in a working-class family on the outskirts of London during the 1960s, 70s and 80s. Our mother was a homemaker and was always there before and after school. She nourished our minds, bodies and souls – a strong matriarch, a family-oriented woman who held her children, family and friends close to her. My father worked for London Transport as a train driver. He instilled in us the importance of a good education and the ethos to always work hard. Although our parents rarely attended parents' evenings or got involved in school activities, we all did well at school. When I say well, I mean we had good attendance records, achieved solid academic results and secured places in further education that resulted in corporate careers.

My career started in the Information Technology (IT) department at an airline as a technical specialist working on installing and fixing computer hardware and software, progressing to project management design. I moved into 'Learning and Development', where I was responsible for large teams of IT staff as a resource manager. My primary areas of focus were career development, health and wellbeing, role assignment and performance.

Listen closely

My children were born and raised throughout my working life. First, a girl, Lynnette, then a boy and, finally, twins, a boy and a girl. Lynnette was an only child for five years before her brother came along. It was another three years before the twins were born. Four children under ten was tough, but I managed with the support of my husband and family. We had childminders and a live-in and live-out au pair to support us with childcare while my husband and I worked full-time to provide for our family. We had a good life. We both worked hard, and I was able to progress in my career, enabling us to improve our standard of living as the years passed.

When Lynnette was in school, it was identified that she struggled to concentrate in class and was not progressing at the rate expected. After assessment by the school educational psychologist, we learned she was dyslexic. She was entitled to and given a 'statement', now called the Educational Health Care Plan (EHCP) – we will discuss this in more detail later in the book.

My initial reaction was guilt. What had I done wrong? I was focused on developing my career to be able to support our family and have a decent standard of living. It was important that I constantly developed my skills and excelled in the workplace. I can see how this could be perceived as selfishness, and I some-times questioned myself, but in my mind, the reason for developing my career was to benefit my family long-term.

Meetings with teachers to identify strategies for helping Lynnette's progress usually ended with me in tears. I had no idea how to deal with the situa-tion or who to turn to for advice. This was in the late 1980s and early 1990s. I felt ashamed. It was my fault; I hadn't been spending enough time with my daughter. I didn't share her challenges with my wider family. My husband and I did our best, imple-menting the strategies suggested by the school. But we didn't do any additional research beyond that which the school and educational psychologist had provided, and we did not truly understand what the disorder meant for my daughter or what the impact on her was.

As a result, my daughter struggled to communi-cate with me. She rebelled, displaying challenging behaviour to get the attention she craved from me. Of course, I wanted the best for her, but I did not spend enough time trying to understand what was happening to her. As she got older, this resulted in behaviour that caused conflict between us. On one occasion, we thought we were giving her responsi-bility by allowing her to stay at home rather than come on a family holiday. She held a full-blown house party, removing all the furniture from the house. I remember noticing that things were not quite right when we returned, before getting the lowdown from the neighbour who, of course, told us everything. On another occasion, as she neared seventeen, she ran away from home for three days. I was beside myself with worry – none of our family or friends knew where she was. Eventually, she returned and, with a friend supporting us, we were able to talk through her reasons for leaving and coaxed her back home. I now realise these outbursts were cries for help. Cries that I did not hear. She wanted to communicate her struggles but did not know how to. I was so focused on my career and my other three children that I did not give Lynnette the time she needed. I did not listen closely enough to hear what she was trying to tell me. Despite these early challenges, as Lynnette matured and had her own family, we became close.

It is difficult to open my heart in this way, but I recognise that other parents relate to my journey and value the insight.

Lynnette's story

Lynnette left school with a few GCSEs but no clear direction. After a few office jobs, she developed a passion for working with disadvantaged young people, those who were homeless, single parents or NEET (not in education, employment or training). She excelled in this field as she felt a connection to them and could relate to their situation.

Although we'd had a turbulent relationship during her teenage years, when Lynnette turned nineteen everything seemed to change. We spent a lot of time together, talking about what she was doing work wise, and I helped her with job applications, motivating her when she was down and celebrating her successes. Lynnette is now mother to four children. She was thirty-two when she had Mekhi, her third child and oldest son. When he was small, she had a strong social network consisting of friends and family members whom she met with regularly. Many of them were also new parents and they would meet up on their own and with their children. I loved knowing that she had friends outside our relationship. Although dyslexic, Lynnette had grown into a strong, confident verbal communicator. Her natural warmth and ability to connect with people gained her a wide and varied circle of friends and acquaintances. I could see that it was important to her to have close connections with people who understood the challenges of life, and parenthood.

As Mekhi got older, his behaviour started to change, and he became more boisterous. The other children in Lynnette's social network did not like being around him. His behaviour had become problematic and learning and behavourial difficulties more pronounced. He was attending appointments for speech therapy, assessments with psychologists and pae-diatricians, as well as with other professionals. The challenges of caring for a young child with learn-ing and behavioural difficulties were beginning to surface. Almost daily, Lynnette would be told of an issue with her son's behaviour at nursery, of what he had done to another child, or that he had fallen over again.

Lynnette had made a decision early on that she would focus on her children over her career, even if that meant working part-time and struggling finan-cially. Her priority was to give her children what they needed, regardless of the impact on her personal goals, and she would do whatever it took. At a time when Mekhi needed an increasing amount of time and attention, Lynnette took redundancy to focus on supporting him – and for the sake of her mental health and wellbeing. It was around this time that I noticed that she no longer had that wide circle of friends. As Mekhi had got older, her social network had reduced.

Home life for Lynnette and her family was impacted by Mekhi's behaviour. His siblings were frustrated with his tantrums, outbursts and that he often received more attention than they did from their mum. It was clear to me that she was struggling to cope with all the demands placed on her and we finally had the con-versation that brought to light what was happening with Mekhi and the strain it was putting on her, her relationships and her family. She had been trying to deal with Mekhi totally alone.

Talking to Lynnette about Mekhi's learning and development in an attempt to better understand their situation, I asked what information she had about his condition and what research she had done. She handed me a file about four inches thick. It contained all the letters and results from the tests they had undertaken. I was astounded. My daughter, who had her own learning challenges, had been dealing with this situation alone, trying to make sense of everything.

Having supported the homeless, jobless, parents and youth for years in her job, Lynnette had experienced first-hand some of the possible outcomes for young people when they don't have the right support. As a result, she was keen to ensure that her son received the support and education required to make sure he did not tread the lonely, sad, dangerous path that she had seen so many young people follow.

I so admire the tenacity and strength of character she has shown in all she has achieved; despite the challenges she has faced. She is a true mamma bear, protecting her young whatever they go through, putting her family first and foremost. As her mum, she and I had our disputes and misunderstandings while she was growing up, but when she became a parent, she gained insight that helped her to realise why certain decisions about her upbringing were made. She then blossomed into the beautiful daughter and parent that I am so proud of today.

Despite this, as I learned more about her current situation, I had feelings of guilt and remorse. As a life coach, I tend to look forward, helping my clients to recognise what they have and work towards the future they desire. In this instance, I had to stop focusing on myself and figure out what I could do to help my daughter move forward. Not only was this an opportunity for me to step up and give her the support that perhaps I could have done years previously, I had the ability to make a real difference to my grandson's life.

Please note, Lynnette's is not a sad tale. It is a story that will resonate with many parents. It is happening now, all over the place. This book aims to help you realise that you are not alone, to provide inspiration and education about supporting a child or children with ADHD and other similar and/or related conditions.

Listen to your child

The first step in supporting your child with ADHD is to *listen* to your child. Observe them in their daily life. Find out how they operate and what their strengths are. Record what you see happening around them. Gathering evidence and information is crucial at this stage because, as you go deeper into seeking support for your child, this information will be invaluable. Keeping a diary is a good place to start.

AN INTERVIEW WITH LYNNETTE – AUGUST 2019

Something different

'When Mekhi was around two years old, I noticed his level of communication was not where it should be. His behaviour would easily and quickly spiral out of control. He was not able to say what was wrong or what he wanted. I knew this wasn't right. He was constantly hyper and on the go. He had lots of tantrums and I didn't know what to do to control his behaviour. He constantly needed interaction. When he got worked up, he couldn't talk or communicate with me.'

His behaviour

'He would quickly get angry and throw things around. He would spit at me, punch me and tell me he didn't love me if I told him off. His behaviour was different to that of his older siblings when they were his age. Mekhi took longer to settle, and his sleep was erratic. He often would not go to sleep at night and then would not get up in the morning for school because he was so tired. I noticed that his speech was difficult to understand. He could not communicate what he was feeling and would get frustrated. He would have outbursts that seemed to come from nowhere, I would have no idea what triggered them.'

Mekhi at pre-school

'Mekhi went to nursery for a while. When he was three, he started going to pre-school. It was picked up there that he was always bumping into the other kids and falling over. I talked to the school about his speech delay and they confirmed that he was not where he should be on the scale. The pre-school worked in partnership with speech and language therapists and Mekhi was assessed and put on a special programme. Although the pre-school put in place the interventions suggested to help with his development, little progress was made. I could see that the school was struggling to manage his behaviour; every day they would report something to me, either he had pushed another child or something else had happened. They didn't question why he was doing these things and no support was given. That's when I decided to take him out of the pre-school and not to send him to the school attached to it, as I didn't believe that they would be able to support him appropriately either. I found another local school that had the resources to support children with additional needs, they also had a speech and language department.

This was the start of the journey toward understanding that Mekhi was a bit different and required more support in some areas. He could not feed himself or put his coat on and he was always falling over. In hindsight, there were so many signs, but I'd found it difficult to spot them. I was always told that boys are a little slower in their development; he was my first boy and so I initially thought it was normal.'

Impact on the family

'His older sisters found Mekhi frustrating. He needed a lot of attention, while they were used to getting all the attention themselves. They were having to do basic things for him because he couldn't manage himself. His behaviour would spiral out of control and they did not want to be around him.'

How Lynnette felt

'I was upset and frustrated. I wondered what I had done wrong, what I had done differently with my previous two children. I didn't know what to do. Would he grow out of it? Was it genetics? I felt paralysed, thinking about what to do next. I found it difficult to access any support. Mekhi was seen simply as a naughty boy with behaviour problems. I felt alone and helpless. I hoped that when he got to the new school, with all their resources, things would be OK.'

Mekhi at primary school

'Mekhi was four when he started primary school, the youngest in his class of thirty children. The first two terms were fine. He was able to participate and he enjoyed going to school. I thought he was doing well. I hadn't received any negative feedback from anyone until, one day, his teacher pulled me aside after school and said, "I think you should get Mekhi assessed for developmental delay." I knew he was behind but had no idea what she was talking about. He was still only four, in reception. She was a wonderful young teacher; Mekhi loved her, everything about her was just what he needed. I could see that she cared about Mekhi. She said that she had raised her concerns but that

I needed to speak with the school myself to get him assessed. She told me exactly what I needed to do to get support for Mekhi in school; without her assistance, I would not have been aware of what he needed or how to get it. This teacher continued to support Mekhi and gave me resources so that I could help him at home, resources that helped with his motor skills and for learning shapes, letters and numbers. I don't think the school had any idea she put these materials together for me.'

Hearing about the support Lynnette received from this teacher lifted my spirits; it was good to know there are teachers out there who really care about their pupils. As parents, we rely on schools and what they tell us. If this teacher had not pulled Lynnette aside, she would not have been aware of what Mekhi's needs were. The teacher informed Lynnette that children were usually assessed between the ages of six and twelve. How fortunate for Mekhi that his teacher was on the ball and prepared to go the extra lengths to support his learning and development in his first year at school.

Tips for listening to your child

Listening is a skill that needs to be developed, especially as we are aiming to learn and gather information to help make decisions or perhaps calm a child that is upset. Sometimes you need to listen for what is not being said by observing body language and other external cues.

There are different types of listening styles, and you may adopt some or all depending on the circumstance.[1]

- Passive listening – there is no interaction using this approach:
  - Listen to the tone of voice being used
  - Allow your child to speak without interrupting them
  - Do not react to what is being said
- Attentive listening – there may be some interaction using this approach:
  - There is some verbal conversation taking place
  - Acknowledge the comments made by your child
  - Use your body language to show you are listening ie nodding
  - Give feedback but avoid judgement
- Active listening – there is a high level of interaction using this approach: similar to attentive listening with more interactions:
  - More verbal exchange and a full conversation

---

1   Team Technology, www.teamtechnology.co.uk/soft-skills/project-management-training-part5.html, accessed 18 March 2021

- Observe their body language – non-verbal communication (eg what do they do with their hands when sad or angry?)

- Observe the language, tone and reactions used to what is said – eg aggressive, swear, loud

Ask open questions – to gain information so that you can really hear what is going on for your child and help you raise a point or gain clarity on a situation:

- What is going on for you?

- How does it feel for you?

- How can I help you?

Once you have asked a question, give your child a chance to digest it and answer.

Repeat back what they say, this shows you have heard them and confirms you heard what they said.

Ask for examples so you fully understand what they mean, for example, 'You say you get distracted in class, tell me what that looks like, how do you feel when that happens?' Gradually add other questions to gather as much information as you can, for example, 'What have you tried to stop it happening?' 'What do you enjoy about the lessons you get distracted in?' 'What do you dislike about the lessons you get distracted in?'

2
Conduct Your Own Research

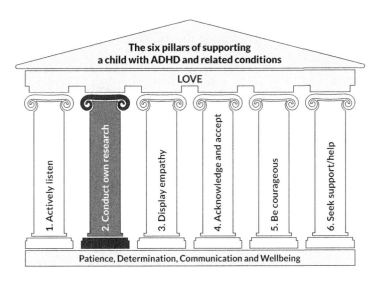

The six pillars of supporting
a child with ADHD and related conditions

LOVE

1. Actively listen

2. Conduct own research

3. Display empathy

4. Acknowledge and accept

5. Be courageous

6. Seek support/help

Patience, Determination, Communication and Wellbeing

On learning of the challenges faced by my daughter and grandson, I had no idea where to start with trying to understand exactly what was going on. My daughter had given me a huge pile of documents she had gathered from the school, doctor and other professionals. Reviewing the information, there were lots of acronyms and language that I did not understand: communication from different professionals, forms to be completed, appointments and letters. I sat back in awe at the struggle my daughter faced. With her dyslexia, she must have felt overwhelmed but, as a loving mother, knew she had to do what was required to get support for her child.

The second pillar of the APD process is all about conducting research and educating yourself so that you build a good understanding of your child's condition. This way, you know what you are dealing with, the extent of what your child is facing and the impact it will have. You will then understand what you, as their parent or carer, need to find out about. It is important to get to know the subject area and terminology so that you can communicate effectively with others in the field, and to learn as much as you can about your child's condition and the behaviours they display. The second pillar in the APD process gives you some ideas of how to approach this.

It goes without saying that you need to ensure the source of your information is reliable and trustworthy;

this in itself can be a challenge, so below I've included some data and findings from the ADHD Foundation.

THE ADHD FOUNDATION

The ADHD Foundation is based in Liverpool in the UK. It is the largest 'user-led' ADHD agency in Europe and is seen as influencing policy provision in the UK for those living with ADHD and related/similar conditions. There are NHS consultant psychiatrists and paediatricians on its board of directors, as well as service users. It is one of the first charities in the UK to include NHS 'Improved Access to Psychological Therapies'. You can find out more about their services at www.adhdfoundation.org.uk.

In the report *A Lifetime Lost, or A Lifetime Saved: ADHD in children in the UK in 2017*[2] it is highlighted that:

- Up to 30% of children with ADHD may have a separate serious mood disorder such as depression

- Up to 30% of children and over half of adults with ADHD also suffer with an anxiety disorder

- Around a third of people with ADHD have to wait over two years before they are formally diagnosed

2   Finlan O'Regan, Dr Matthew McConkey, Poppy Ellis Logan and Dr Tony Lloyd, *Born to be ADHD: A Lifetime Lost, or a Lifetime Saved,* www.adhdfoundation.org.uk/wp-content/uploads/2017/11/ A-Lifetime-Lost-or-a-Lifetime-Saved-report.pdf (October 2017), accessed 20 March 2021

- Up to 20% of individuals with ADHD may show symptoms of bipolar disorder

- Children with untreated or poorly controlled ADHD are:

  - More than five times more likely to participate in fights

  - More than twice as likely to feel frustrated at school

  - Three times as likely to have a reading disability

The earlier a child is diagnosed, the better the opportunity to put in place the right support mechanisms. Without support, there is an increased risk of mental health problems, substance misuse and offending.[3]

There is a plethora of organisations dedicated to supporting children and adults with ADHD and other conditions. I have found a few in the UK and many in America. Children and Adults with Attention Deficit/Hyperactivity Disorder (CHADD) (www. chadd.org) is an American organisation that provides access to research papers, lots of resources for both children and adults, as well as training and

---

3   Finlan O'Regan, Dr Matthew McConkey, Poppy Ellis Logan and
     Dr Tony Lloyd, *Born to be ADHD: A Lifetime Lost or a Lifetime Saved,*
     www.adhdfoundation.org.uk/wp-content/uploads/2017/11/
     A-Lifetime-Lost-or-a-Lifetime-Saved-report.pdf (October 2017),
     accessed 20 March 2021

access to conferences at reduced rates if you become a member.

In the UK, I've already mentioned the ADHD Foundation. They can carry out full ADHD diagnostic screening for adults and pre-diagnostic screening for children. They also provide a wealth of support and information on their website (www.adhdfoundation. org.uk).

I used both of the above organisations to help with my research on this topic.

The EHCP

My first attempt to understand what was happening involved making sense of the documentation my daughter had given me, which consisted of an EHCP. Due to the insight provided by Mekhi's teacher and the support of the school, Lynnette had been able to have Mekhi assessed. As a result, additional resources and interventions were put in place to ensure that he had the educational support he required. This is not a straightforward process. Once the EHCP has been awarded, you then need to meet with the relevant parties in the school to understand what will be actioned and when. This in itself can be challenging and you may need to chase and push for this meeting to take place. Lynnette's experience has shown me the importance of driving conversations forward, asking all the questions you need to so that you fully understand what is going to be put in place, how progress will be measured and any other clarification you need. There are no stupid questions.

Those with an EHCP may be awarded a Disability Living Allowance (DLA), funding to help with the extra costs associated with resources that may be required to support the individual with their condition.

The above information is not widely known. Among the parents who have attended my support group, those who were aware of their child's learning difficulties had no idea how to go about getting an EHCP for their child. This was not their fault. This information is often not readily available or shared with you unless you pressurise the school or your doctor for help. This is why it is essential to raise awareness of the options open to parents. To request an EHCP from your local authority, you do not require a diagnosis. It is based on your child's educational needs and you need only to be able to demonstrate that your child needs more support than is currently available to them. I have provided a detailed explanation about what an EHCP is, and how to obtain one later in this chapter.

An EHCP for Mekhi

Figure 2.1 shows the journey Lynnette went on to get an EHCP for Mekhi; this may vary depending on where you live. The key point is that there *is* a process, and you can find out about what that is and how long it takes in your area from the school, your doctor or your local authority.

You don't need the support of your school to apply for an EHCP, but it certainly helps. There are 1.1 million children across the UK in mainstream schools with special educational needs (SEN); 12.8% in Primary schools and 11.1% in Secondary schools.[4]

UNDERSTANDING THE EDUCATIONAL HEALTH CARE PLAN (EHCP) PROCESS[5]

In the UK, the EHCP process is managed by your local authority. The focus is the child's educational needs. The EHC Plan will stay with them throughout their education and will provide an insight into their academic ability and development, as assessed by a professional, typically a school psychologist. Families are fully involved in the assessment and planning stages. It should be a collaborative approach with all the relevant specialist teams involved working together to determine and agree the approach and

---

4   Department for Education, 'Special educational needs in England: January 2020 (July 2020), www.gov.uk/government/statistics/special-educational-needs-in-england-january-2020, accessed 20 March 2021

5   EHCP Journeys, https://ehcpjourneys.com, accessed 20 March 2021

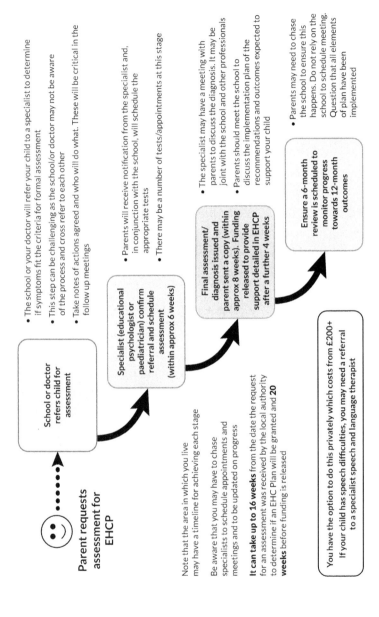

Parent requests assessment for EHCP

School or doctor refers child for assessment

- The school or your doctor will refer your child to a specialist to determine if symptoms fit the criteria for formal assessment
- This step can be challenging as the school and/or doctor may not be aware of the process and cross refer to each other
- Take notes of actions agreed and who will do what. These will be critical in the follow up meetings

Specialist (educational psychologist or paediatrician) confirm referral and schedule assessment (within approx 6 weeks)

- Parents will receive notification from the specialist and, in conjunction with the school, will schedule the appropriate tests
- There may be a number of tests/appointments at this stage

Final assessment/ diagnosis issued and parent sent a copy (within approx 8 weeks). Funding released to provide support detailed in EHCP after a further 4 weeks

- The specialist may have a meeting with parents to discuss the diagnosis. It may be joint with the school and other professionals
- Parents should meet the school to discuss the implementation plan of the recommendations and outcomes expected to support your child

Ensure a 6-month review is scheduled to monitor progress towards 12-month outcomes

- Parents may need to chase the school to ensure this happens. Do not rely on the school to schedule the meeting. Question that all elements of plan have been implemented

Note that the area in which you live may have a timeline for achieving each stage

Be aware that you may have to chase specialists to schedule appointments and meetings and to be updated on progress

It can take up to 16 weeks from the date the request for an assessment was received by the local authority to determine if an EHC Plan will be granted and **20 weeks** before funding is released

You have the option to do this privately which costs from £200+ If your child has speech difficulties, you may need a referral to a specialist speech and language therapist

Figure 2.1 Getting your child assessed for an EHCP

way forward. Should interventions be required by additional professions, this will all be captured within the document. Progress and reviews are part of the process and these meetings should be managed by the local authority.

The EHCP process has five steps. You should check the timescales for your local authority to determine how long each step typically takes in your area.

Step one: Identifying

This is where a need for an assessment is determined and relevant professionals approached. At this stage, you would gather your evidence and submit an application to your local authority.

Step two: Assessing

The local authority considers the application and all the information submitted to determine if there is a case for additional support.

Step three: Planning

Based on all the information gathered so far, the local authority decides what kind of additional support is required, how much support is needed, and how it should be implemented. A plan will be produced which sets out, in detail, the targeted outcomes and how the additional needs will be met.

Step four: Actioning

At this point, the plan is being implemented and the support should be being provided. During the delivery of the plan, the outcomes are monitored against what is set out in the plan.

Step five: Review

A formal review of the EHCP is conducted to determine that progress against the plan is being achieved and, if it is not, agreeing what changes need to be made.

If you need help and support through the EHCP process, contact the Independent Provider of Special Education Advice (IPSEA). They are a registered charity in England and provide free legal information, advice and support. You should also speak to your local SEN co-ordinator, who is usually based in the school, or contact your local authority.

At Mekhi's review meeting the school updated the document initially and the local authority sense checked it prior to issue to the parents for sign-off. As a parent it is vital that you understand in detail what is contained in the document, the work that will be delivered and that it explains clearly the outcomes expected ensuring they are realistic and achievable. You have the ability to challenge the content if you feel information has been left out or does not accurately represent your child's situation. Parents should have access to this document when speaking to a professional about their child as it a legal document and provides a clear record of concerns, actions and outcomes.

Implementing an EHCP

It is important to consider that, although you may be successful in obtaining an EHCP, it then needs to be implemented and progress monitored. Six months after Mekhi got his EHCP, Lynnette found that, although the recommendations made in the plan had been implemented, there had been little progress in Mekhi's learning. She had concerns about the way in which certain recommendations were being implemented and the fact that how his progress would be monitored and reported had not been agreed.

As your child's advocate, you need to know what suggestions have been made in the EHCP, which of these have been implemented and what improvements have been seen. Ensure you have an agreement in place for how frequently you will check in with the school, teacher, SEN and head teacher to be updated on your child's progress. When monitoring the implementation of the EHCP, things to pay attention to and enquire about include:

- How well-equipped the school is to implement the recommendations

- What skills the staff have in implementing these kinds of interventions

- How the suggestions are being applied in school and how your child is adapting

- How your child's progress will be measured, including how this measurement tool or method is going to be used and how successful it has been in the past

- If what is implemented is not having a positive impact on your child, it should be reviewed and adapted as appropriate

- Keep an open dialogue with all parties, agree a communication approach and follow up if it is not being adhered to

Diagnosis and symptoms

Once Mekhi had his diagnosis of ADHD, dyspraxia and development delay, we then needed to understand what this meant. ADHD is a medical condition that affects behaviour. The brain development and brain activity is different in a person with ADHD; this affects their attention span, their ability to sit still and their self-control.[6] Some common symptoms of ADHD include:

- Unable to stay focused on one thing

- Constant fidgeting or moving about – unable to sit still to eat or have a book read to them

- Excessive talking and making a lot of noise

---

6 Radboud University Nijmegen Medical Centre, 'Brain differences in ADHD' (ScienceDaily, 16 February 2017), www.sciencedaily.com/releases/2017/02/170216105919.htm, accessed 20 March 2021

It is important to remember that each child is different, and the severity of their symptoms will differ, as will their triggers. My daughter and I noticed that when Mekhi had food with a high sugar content, his symptoms were heightened, and he became more boisterous and impulsive. Seek professional advice from a doctor, and perhaps a nutritionist, who specialises in your child's condition to help you decide the best course of action to take for your child.

DIET AND ADHD

Dorothy Mullen wrote an interesting article on diet and its impact on ADHD, *Helping People Establish Healthy Eating Habits* that you may find helpful.[7] Food is not a cause of ADHD, but some people find certain foods seem to make symptoms worse. Be sure to speak to your doctor or a nutritionist before changing your child's diet or giving them any supplements.

Dyspraxia, also known as developmental co-ordination disorder (DCD), is a condition that affects motor skills and is a comorbid condition of ADHD. People with dyspraxia can struggle with balance and physical co-ordination and Mekhi was finding it difficult to dress himself, tie his shoelaces and other activities that required fine motor skills. He appeared to be clumsy, constantly bumping into other children

---

7   D Mullen, 'Helping People Establish Healthy Eating Habits', CHADD (*Attention Magazine*, June 2012), https://chadd.org/attention-article/helping-people-establish-healthy-eating-habits, accessed 25 February 2021

and falling over. He struggled to learn to ride a bike. At one stage, he was sleeping for long periods of time and it was difficult to get him up for school in the morning. These are all symptoms of dyspraxia.[8]

Comorbid conditions for ADHD

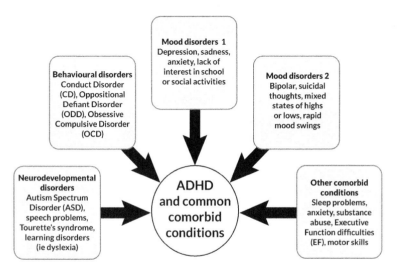

Figure 2.2 High level view of related conditions to ADHD

Figure 2.2 shows the additional conditions that can be linked to ADHD, which sit in four main areas: neurodevelopmental disorders, behavioural disorders, mood disorders and other comorbid conditions. A child may have one or more of these conditions and

---

8   Ann Pietrangelo, 'How dyspraxia differs from other development delays in children' (*healthline*, 26 September 2019), www.healthline.com/health/dyspraxia#risk-factors, accessed 20 March 2021

the severity of each condition will vary from child to child. In addition to ADHD, Mekhi had speech problems, learning disorders, mild symptoms of depression, occasional Oppositional Defiant Disorder (ODD), sleep problems and dyspraxia.

I have coached children who have been diagnosed with autism. They have typically had few friends, lacked emotional expression, been anxious about their health and wellbeing and suffered with anxiety.

To diagnose a condition is a challenge when so many factors need to be considered. Because symptoms can be similar to or masked by other symptoms, it's possible to miss something and not get the diagnosis right first time. As Mekhi matured, his symptoms and behaviours changed, with some diminishing and others becoming more intense.

SYMPTOMS OF ADHD AND COMORBID CONDITIONS

Below are some of the common symptoms and behaviours of ADHD and several other comorbid and related conditions. Remember, every child is different and a diagnosis of one of these conditions doesn't necessarily mean your child will experience all of the associated symptoms. Conditions may present differently in different individuals and the severity of symptoms can vary. Girls can also present differently to boys.

ADHD[9]

- Forgetful, lose things
- Considered 'naughty' by those who do not understand the condition
- Unable to control behaviour or actions
- Feel upset if and when they cause upset to others
- Suffer extreme emotions
- Have low self-confidence; may feel isolated by their peers
- Can be labelled a 'troublemaker'
- Find it difficult to sit still – young children may be overly boisterous, adults highly active
- Suffer tiredness and difficulty sleeping
- Can be easily distracted and unable to concentrate or focus
- Meltdowns and tantrums are commonplace and may become violent as child gets older
- Talks incessantly, quickly and may muddle words; can be loud/noisy
- Does not consider consequences; does things without thinking or understanding danger

Dyslexia[10]

- Problems identifying speech sounds
- Difficulties sounding out certain letters
- Uses the incorrect word when referring to something

---

9   CHADD, 'About ADHD – Overview', https://chadd.org/about-adhd/overview, accessed 19 April 2021
10   Mayo Clinic, 'Dyslexia', www.mayoclinic.org/diseases-conditions/dyslexia/symptoms-causes/syc-20353552, accessed 19 April 2021

- Difficulties with accurate and fluent word recognition
- Challenges with spelling and reading

Oppositional Defiant Disorder (ODD)[11]

- Hostile, disobedient and defiant behaviours directed at adults or authority figures
- Angry and irritable moods
- Argumentative and vindictive behaviours
- Deliberately annoying people around them
- Blaming others for their behaviour

Dyspraxia[12]

- Poor balance; seen as clumsy
- Bumps into things and people
- Struggles to tie shoelaces, put on clothes
- Tiredness

You'll notice that some of these symptoms and behaviours are common to more than one condition. This can make diagnosis difficult and confusing. During my research, I quickly realised that there was some overlap between related conditions; I created a chart (Figure 2.3) to help me identify these common features.

---

11 Mayo Clinic, 'Oppositional defiant disorder (ODD)', www.mayoclinic. org/diseases-conditions/oppositional-defiant-disorder/symptoms-causes/syc-20375831, accessed 19 April 2021
12 NHS, 'Development co-ordination disorder (dyspraxia) in children', www.nhs.uk/conditions/developmental-coordination-disorder-dyspraxia/symptoms, accessed 19 April 2021

Symptom	ADHD	Autism	Dyspraxia
Forgetfulness/loses things	✔		✔
Difficulty concentrating/easily distracted/struggles to stay focused	✔		✔
Fidgets/finds it difficult to sit still/bumps into things	✔		✔
Suffers with anxiety/gets upset/cries loudly/has tantrums	✔	✔	
Struggles to cope with change	✔	✔	
Struggles to read facial expressions and gestures of others		✔	
Doesn't show facial expression/struggles to communicate with others		✔	
Avoids eye contact (although may still be listening)		✔	
Has low self-confidence and low self-esteem	✔	✔	✔
Prefers own company/prefers to play with things rather than with others		✔	
Clumsy/poor coordination/struggles to get dressed, tie shoelaces		✔	✔
Has problems with sound, light, touch, smell, taste	✔	✔	✔
Difficulties learning to read and write/handwriting untidy	✔	✔	✔
Sleep issues/not going to sleep/tired in the morning	✔	✔	

This list is not exhaustive. Diagnosis by an experienced professional is required. Seek advice or a referral from your doctor.

Figure 2.3 A guide to common symptoms

Applying your knowledge

Learning about ADHD, related conditions, the possible symptoms and recommended treatments was challenging and often confusing. The more research I did, the more I was bombarded with suggestions and hypotheses about what could help with symptoms. It was overwhelming. I decided to take a step back and shift my focus to my grandson and what he specifically was experiencing.

ALL ABOUT MEKHI AT SIX YEARS OLD

It is one thing to research the facts about a condition or diagnosis but understanding how the person with that condition feels is equally important. My daughter has given me permission to include these responses given by Mekhi and recorded by his paediatrician and educational psychologist during his EHCP assessment.

In response to the question, 'What is important to me?', Mekhi responded that he:

- Likes eating lots
- Enjoys playing computer games
- Loves watching films
- Enjoys colouring

In identifying the challenges Mekhi faced, it was established that these included:

- A difficulty in understanding boundaries
- A difficulty to communicate needs and wants
- A difficulty in maintaining self-care, including dressing, washing and so on
- An inability to recognise danger

Such challenges often led to:

- Unpredictable behaviour
- A tendency towards over-emotional responses
- Frustration

Mekhi did not talk until he was four years old and required intensive speech therapy. He needed support to regulate his behaviour and emotions and help with his communication. The following steps were identified as being helpful in Mekhi's development:

- The breakdown of instructions into small steps
- Building the number of steps incrementally as sometimes there was difficulty in following two-step instructions
- Repetitive learning
- Visuals and kinaesthetic prompts to keep responses in context and relevant
- Praise and reward charts, such as smiley faces, to help with self-regulation
- The use of 'traffic lights' to reflect mood and behaviour

Professional input such as this is invaluable. Mekhi's early years teacher, for example, was the person who first helped his mum understand the challenges he faced. The more open and honest this teacher was about what was happening with him, the easier Lynnette found it to take on board the information and take appropriate action. Of course, it was daunting and emotional at times, but having this insight helped Lynnette to deal with the situation. It provided her with information that she would need later to get the right support for Mekhi.

Talking to your child's teacher, listening to what they say and being open to what they suggest is critical in building up a picture of their daily life at school. What might seem like a small, one-off occurrence that can be ignored or brushed off as a minor incident, could be part of a bigger issue. If Lynnette had not been open to listening to and communicating with Mekhi's teacher, she would not have gained such useful insight into her son's days at school, insight that enabled her to monitor and compare his behaviour at home. This information is important to have when it comes to seeking assessment, as your child must be displaying symptoms in two or more settings, eg at home and at school.

ADHD IN GIRLS

As I mentioned, ADHD and related conditions often present differently in girls compared to boys and, as a result, girls with ADHD are often not diagnosed until they are older.[13] I know of girls who were not diagnosed until their mid to late teenage years. A friend's daughter was not diagnosed until she reached university.

---

13 Maureen Connolly, 'ADHD in girls: Why it's ignored, why that's dangerous', *ADDitude: Inside the ADHD mind* (2 October 2019), www. additudemag.com/adhd-in-girls-women, accessed 20 March 2021

Listed are some common signs and symptoms of ADHD in girls. It is important to note that only an experienced professional can diagnose the condition; if you are concerned that your child may be showing any of these symptoms on a regular basis, seeking the advice of a professional would be advisable.

Girls with ADHD can often:

- Appear withdrawn
- Cry and be upset easily
- Daydream and seem in a world of their own
- Find it difficult to maintain focus and be easily distracted
- Give the impression they are not trying
- Seem unmotivated
- Be forgetful
- Be overly talkative
- Make careless mistakes
- Slam doors
- Be late
- Not complete tasks
- Appear to be shy
- Appear not to hear instructions or take a while to understand

This list is not exhaustive; it is just an example of the types of behaviours that sometimes get missed in girls.[14]

---

14 Keath Low, '20 signs and symptoms of ADHD in girls: How the condition tends to present in females may surprise you', *verywellmind* (18 November 2020) www.verywellmind.com/adhd-in-girls-symptoms-of-adhd-in-girls-20547, accessed 20 March 2021

Observing your child at home

It's helpful to spend time observing your child's behaviour over a period of time and noting down what you notice. This will help you establish whether the behaviour is typical of children within your child's peer group, or whether your child is indeed displaying behaviours that are associated with these conditions.

Mekhi is the third of four children and wants to be included in whatever is going on. When his baby brother came along, we could not leave Mekhi alone in the room with him. Although to Mekhi he was just playing, he could not regulate his strength and did not understand that a baby could not do the things he wanted to do. It was much safer to keep them apart, even when his brother was a toddler.

We now use different strategies (discussed later in the book) to regulate his behaviour at home, especially when he is playing with his brother or other children, and these have worked well. He has learned to ride a bike, swim and participates in martial arts. These activities are particularly good for him, as they involve exercise and require discipline and structure.

These insights and observations have helped us to understand Mekhi and are important parts of the research we needed to gain a big picture view of his condition, how it impacts him and how to communicate with him effectively. If I had taken the same time to understand my daughter's challenges when she was younger, we may not have had so much conflict.

Tips for parenting a child with ADHD

ADHD is believed to be hereditary, but the way that your child's symptoms are managed can have a major effect on their severity and what other problems may occur. Early identification is critical to enabling your child to have a positive outcome and achieve their potential. When Mekhi is told off, he takes it to heart, and it can take a lot of explaining to get him to understand why he has been disciplined. If not addressed, these negative feelings can lead to poor self-esteem and anti-social behaviour.

There are several things you can do to help your child improve their skills and have a happier life at home and at school:

- **Identify the things they are good at** and interested in and support them in continuing to develop in those areas. Notice when they behave appropriately and tell them exactly what they did well.

- Continue to **develop your knowledge** about your child's condition and what help they are entitled to. This will help you ensure you get the best support at an important time of their development while they're in education.

- Continually **tell your child you love and support them always**. This may not always be easy to do but letting them know you are on their side and there for them is powerful and will help to build their self-esteem.

- Have your child **fully assessed**, including for any comorbid conditions, so that you have a full picture of their diagnosis.

- Help your child to make and understand friendships and how to work with others, so that they **develop social skills**.

- **Keep records** of all the information you gather from school and other professionals, and observations of your child's behaviour and challenges.

- Ensure all the **relevant people attend formal meetings and provide input**. Insist on this and prepare beforehand.

- Aim to **work collaboratively with your school** and local authority; you want them to become part of the team that is supporting your child. Communicate regularly with your child's teacher and support staff so you can keep track of progress and quickly address any issues that arise.

- **Explain how to manage your child to all** the people who may come into contact with them; it is important that you work together.

- As ADHD can be hereditary, it might be useful to **find out if you have it** and address any issues that may arise. This could improve the home environment, introducing a calmer lifestyle.

- **Discipline is important**. Implementing a reward system will not only help teach appropriate behaviours, it will enable your child to understand that there are consequences for behaving inappropriately. Ensure the strategies used are applied consistently by everyone your child is in contact with.

3
Display Empathy

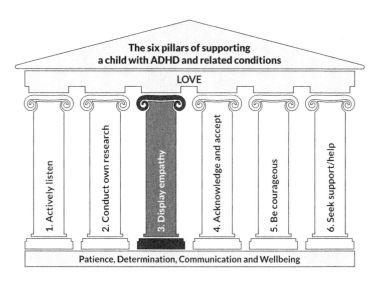

The six pillars of supporting
a child with ADHD and related conditions

LOVE

1. Actively listen

2. Conduct own research

3. Display empathy

4. Acknowledge and accept

5. Be courageous

6. Seek support/help

Patience, Determination, Communication and Wellbeing

This chapter is all about having a good understanding of what someone with ADHD and related conditions is going through; what emotions they are experiencing, and the challenges they face in managing those emotions. We'll talk about how the brain of someone with ADHD and/or related conditions functions a little differently to that of someone who does not. Insight into these challenges and differences will help move through the APD Process – and to display empathy.

When my daughter Lynnette was young, she often found it difficult to communicate how she felt and would misbehave as a way to get the attention she needed. I was a young mum who lacked an understanding of emotional intelligence and did not spend sufficient quality time with Lynnette, which in her teenage years resulted in conflict and arguments.

My grandson, Mekhi, is highly emotional. There are times when he believes that the action his mum has taken means she does not love him. This quickly escalates into him shouting and crying uncontrollably. The reason for this is twofold: he does not understand that what his mum has done or asked is reasonable; he struggles to regulate his emotions and reacts in an extreme way. Sometimes, he says hurtful things to his mum, which often ends in him being sent to bed rather than a quiet conversation about what has happened.

Some children grow out of having tantrums. Others will continue with this behaviour as they grow up. A small child with ADHD can be highly sensitive. If your child feels you have upset them, this can trigger an outburst of tears, verbal and/or physical aggression and other negative behaviour.

As a parent, it can be a real challenge to consistently follow an empathetic approach. Managing the household, the family, work and social events along with the impact of your child's condition is not easy. You come home from a stressful day at work, you pick up your child from the childminder, they cry all the way home, and nothing soothes them. Their tantrum continues into the house. You try to make the evening meal and get your child to eat through their crying. Then it is bedtime, which does not go smoothly. Trying to control your emotions in this situation is a huge challenge – it would be for anyone. Anger and frustration can appear, which can result in harsh words spoken to a child that can cause damage.

Emotional intelligence

Emotional intelligence (EI, or sometimes EQ) is: an awareness of others' and one's own emotions and the ability to control and express them judiciously when dealing with others. Why is emotional intelligence important to successfully parent a child with ADHD and/or related conditions? As the parent or carer, you are responsible for managing your behaviour. It is critical that you are able to demonstrate empathy and emotional intelligence to your child.

To establish and maintain a positive relationship with your child, it is important that you under-stand what emotions and feelings they are expe-riencing, and what is important to them, as this is what drives their behaviours. Feelings are just as important as emotions – many decisions will be made based on how a child feels about themselves, the task they are approaching, or who is commu-nicating with them. When conflict is experienced, this is usually because emotions and/or feelings are being ignored. This conflict can be between siblings, between parent and child, between a child and their teachers, for example.

As well as your own emotional intelligence, you must also consider the emotional intelligence of your child with ADHD and/or related condition. As humans, the ability to recognise different emotions is essen-tial for building healthy, positive relationships; if we lack this ability, we can encounter problems. People with ADHD and/or related conditions not only find it difficult to recognise their own or others' emotions, they also find it difficult to regulate their emotions, making them prone to extreme responses. Children with ADHD typically struggle with emotional intelligence, which is why they are often excluded by their peers and bullied for being different, or are deemed to lack the ability to concentrate, listen or pay attention. They can find it difficult to read facial cues, expressions and emotion, and also to display emotion themselves. This will impact their ability to make friends and establish relationships. It is important for a parent to understand this in order to help their child.

I remember frequently having to go into school to discuss concerns about my daughter's behaviour, her academic progress, or her development. It was an incredibly hard thing to do. My priority was always to do the best I could and get the support she needed but keeping my emotions in check was almost impossible. I know this is a challenge for many parents in similar situations – I see it a lot in ADHD support groups on social media, and my own support group where parents can be so emotional in meetings that they find it hard to communicate effectively.

Not being able to control your emotions makes it difficult to have a clear and coherent conversation where you share your ideas, thoughts and suggestions in an organised way. This can make you feel vulnerable. I certainly felt vulnerable. Although I was in a good job, leading and managing teams of people, when it came to dealing with the school and my children, I fell apart. This was in part due to my lack of emotional intelligence, but also due to my lack of knowledge about what I was dealing with. My primary source of information was the school and their psychologist. Building my career and supporting my family were my primary focus; the internet was in its infancy and I had no time to go to the library and do extra research. I had never dealt with the local authority and felt powerless to challenge or question the school – I had been brought up in a time where you didn't question or challenge the education system.

My daughter, on the other hand, due to her profession, had experience of dealing with government organisations, local authorities and service providers, and of course had access to resources not available to me. She has a certain degree of insider knowledge not available to most parents. This often comes to light in our support group meetings, where she is able to share insights and give examples of situations from firsthand experience. Working with single parents and the homeless has required her to help young people gain access to support and benefits, often having to challenge organisations to achieve this.

Lynnette has a high level of emotional intelligence. She regularly demonstrates her exceptional ability to communicate effectively with well-structured arguments and clearly articulated ideas. She has told me that there have been moments when she's wanted to just sit and cry – and I'm sure, on occasion, she has – but her courage and commitment to her son outweigh everything and so her fight continues. She has always been able to identify with the people she works with. Her own struggles have enabled her to understand on a deep and personal level the feelings of her clients and of the parents in our support group. She has been there, felt it, worked through it, and continues to work hard to help her son.

I am on a journey of self-discovery. Learning more about my daughter, what she went through and is still going through now, I feel fortunate that she no longer holds how I dealt with her situation against me. At one time she did. She tried to tell me how she felt, but until now I did not understand. In my eyes, I had done everything I could to support her. She felt I could have done more, and it took me a long time to acknowledge that. There is a sense of relief in letting go of my ego, which hadn't allowed me to think that I was a bad mother. I wasn't a bad mother. I just didn't have the emotional intelligence, at the time, to recognise her suffering.

FIVE WAYS TO DEVELOP YOUR EMOTIONAL INTELLIGENCE (FOR PARENTS)

Living with ADHD is a challenge for parents. When you are able to manage and reduce your negative emotions, you are less likely to get overwhelmed. This is important because our children watch and learn from our behaviours and reactions. Below are five tips on how you can develop your EI and set a good example:

1. **Stay calm when you are feeling frustrated.** Appearing calm and not shouting will help those around you to remain calm also.

2. **Use positive language – both verbal and non-verbal.** Communicate the inappropriate behaviour you want to change by highlighting the appropriate behaviour. Be aware of your own body language. Both verbal and non-verbal language may impact those around you.

3. **Identify your stressors.** When you know what causes your stress you can then work to reduce it.

4. **Be courageous.** Finding strength and courage when things get tough is an important energy for you to harness in yourself and others enabling you to be successful.

5. **Focus on the lessons learned.** Demonstrating a positive approach to managing challenging situations will keep the focus on acknowledging what has occurred and considering improvements that can be implemented in the future.

Emotions, exercise and the ADHD brain

Doctor John Ratey, an American medical doctor and ADHD expert, has written about exercise and ADHD for ADDitude Magazine.[15] In the article, he talks about one of his patients, a twenty-one-year-old man, Jackson, with ADHD who began running almost every day. Jackson said that he'd worked out that when he exercised, he didn't have trouble concentrating on anything. He had originally been on medication for his condition, which he took throughout his school years. He had been disruptive and would not complete his class work. Despite this, Jackson had achieved reasonable grades at school and was looking forward to attending college. During the summer term one year, he discovered a love of running. It helped him to focus and so his grades improved. He was able to concentrate on things that were important to him. Eventually, he decided to come off his medication as he felt so good.

Exercise increases the production of the neurotransmitters dopamine and norepinephrine, both of which are important in regulating the attention system. When you exercise regularly, the baseline levels of dopamine and norepinephrine are raised, which prompts the growth of new receptors in certain brain areas.

15   John Ratey, 'The ADHD exercise solution', *ADDitude: Inside the ADHD Mind* (no date), www.additudemag.com/the-adhd-exercise-solution, accessed 20 March 2021

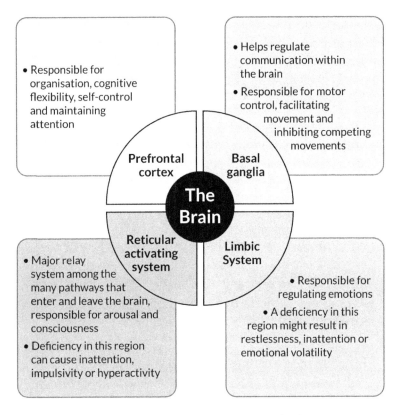

Figure 3.1 How ADHD affects the brain

The **brain stem** is at the bottom end of the brain and is connected to the spinal cord. This area controls the messages sent out to the rest of the body. This is the part of the brain that is involved with psychological responses to stress and panic; it is part of the reticular activating system, our inner radar. Doctor Ratey explains that the **basal ganglia**, a small area that sits within the prefrontal cortex, is responsible for the smooth shifting of the attention system.

Research conducted in America by the University of Georgia found that exercise has an impact on the brain and helps to reduce symptoms of ADHD.[16] According to the study, even small amounts of exercise can help to alleviate the symptoms of ADHD in adults. Taking part in activities with high levels of aerobic activity can help someone with ADHD improve their ability to process information, feel more energised and more motivated to undertake tasks.[17]

Lynnette explored a number of activities for Mekhi; swimming and martial arts have both helped him, as they have a good level of structure with gradually increasing complexity, which keeps him interested. Each child or adult with ADHD is different and the level of attention deficit will vary. It is important to find a solution that works for you and your child.

As parents, we worry about our children all the time, especially when they are young. However, understanding that ADHD is a condition resulting from a malfunction in the way the brain processes information should help you to find solutions that will enable you and your child to cope with the condition. I hope this overview of the role exercise can play in alleviating some common symptoms will help you not only

16 Kathryn M Fritz and Patrick J O'Connor, 'Acute exercise improves mood and motivation in young men with ADHD symptoms', PubMed.gov, 48/6 (June 2016), 1153–60, https://pubmed.ncbi.nlm.nih.gov/26741120, accessed 20 March 2021
17 John Ratey, 'The ADHD exercise solution', *ADDitude: Inside the ADHD Mind* (no date), www.additudemag.com/the-adhd-exercise-solution, accessed 20 March 2021

understand more about the link between ADHD and certain brain functions, but also provide some ideas for activities your child may find fun and exciting.

The CEO of the brain and executive functions

There are seven 'brain skills' that we use to manage everyday functions. These executive functions, imagine them as the CEO of the brain, help us to manage our daily lives. If you have ADHD, there will be a deficit in the way the CEO of your brain, so the executive functions of your brain, operate. The executive functions are:

1. Self-awareness

2. Inhibition

3. Non-verbal working memory

4. Verbal working memory

5. Emotional self-regulation

6. Self-motivation

7. Planning and problem-solving[18]

---

18 Russell Barkely (ed), 'Your child's 7 executive functions – and how to boost them', *ADDittude: Inside the ADHD mind* (12 September 2019), www.additudemag.com/slideshows/boost-executive-function, accessed 20 March 2021

It is important to know the term 'executive functions' and what they are as these functions are key to understanding the struggles your child may have. By being aware of them, you will be able to do your own research into them and delve deeper to understand more about what these functions are and how they impact individuals.

Helping your child manage emotions

As we've already discussed, children with ADHD often do not recognise, or are unable to manage, their emotions. As parents and carers, it is important that we help them to recognise and understand their emotions, and to manage them appropriately. There are many ways to do this. You can use words to describe a particular feeling or emotion and show them what someone expressing that feeling or emotion looks like. For example, you could say, 'I feel sad when you don't share your toys with your brother' and then point out a sad face in a book or on the television or show them what a sad face looks like yourself.

You can talk to your child about how they are feeling, acknowledging their outward displays of emotion. For example, 'You look really happy that we are having ice-cream later on.' Again, use pictures of smiling faces, or show them someone else smiling, so they can see what that emotion looks like. A good example of a feeling to focus on is anger, as this is one that is commonly problematic. Try saying something like, 'I was angry that you lashed out at your brother, it isn't acceptable to lash out at people', and then talk about ways they can calm down if they are feeling angry.

Another thing to talk about is consequences. Explaining to your child what will happen when they display the appropriate behaviours, and what will happen when they don't, will help them to learn how to act. Make sure you give them praise when they do behave appropriately, to reinforce their good behaviour. Identify your child's strengths and focus on them. Show your child you believe in them. Something that can help is creating and using a reward system, which will not only help your child to recognise appropriate behaviour but also incentivise them to display it.

Role modelling is another important strategy, as children often learn how to behave by watching what goes on around them. The way we treat others will indicate to them what behaviours we think are acceptable. Things to consider to ensure you are a good role model for your child are how you treat others around you; how you celebrate your successes and those of others; how you deal with difficult situations; how you support others; how you cope with anger.

Helping with sleep difficulties

Lack of sleep can cause confusion, a bad temper throughout the day and an inability to function effectively. It is important for a child with ADHD and/or related conditions to have a good night's sleep so they can be at their best and make the most of the day ahead; yet sleep is often something they struggle with.

To help address sleep difficulties, it is important to have a regular bedtime routine. Bedtime should be at the same time every day – try and stick to it. As with your morning routine, create a visual showing step by step what things your child needs to do to prepare for bedtime.

The atmosphere in your child's bedroom will contribute significantly to how well they sleep. At bedtime, try to avoid too much noise, though familiar low-level sound, such as a fan, might help them settle and block out any external noises you can't prevent. The scent of lavender is a great relaxant and is often used to aid sleep, so you could try a pillow spray or diffuser.

The hours immediately before bedtime are also important. In particular, you should try to ensure your child does not have access to electronic devices for at least an hour before bedtime – that means no phones, games or TV. This will help their minds to be at rest, which will help them to sleep better. As well as screens, you should avoid or reduce physical activity just before bedtime. In the day though, physical activity will help to burn off excess energy – try not to let them take naps during the day, and they'll sleep more soundly at night. Spending time outside during the day is always a good idea, as fresh air is great for health and wellbeing, which is closely related to sleep.

Instead of digital and physical activities before bedtime, relaxation techniques will help to calm your child down and provide some gentle fun. Try:

- Deep breathing

- Massage

- Listening to calm music

- Reading

- Meditation (more on this in the next section)

It is important for both children with ADHD and their parents to gain a good night's sleep. You will all feel refreshed and better able to manage your day.

Meditation

Meditation is a great tool for helping to calm the mind and improve focus.[19] This might sound like a contradiction for those with active minds, however, with practice it has been found that mindful meditation is an effective method to develop the brain's ability to settle the mind and control attention.[20]

The relaxation exercise below is an introduction to simple meditation techniques:

1. Lie comfortably.

2. Close your eyes.

3. Make no effort to control your breath; simply breathe naturally.

4. Keep your attention on your breath and the movement of your body each time you inhale and exhale. Observe your stomach rise and fall. As you breathe in your stomach rises, as you breathe out your stomach falls. Do not attempt to control the pace or intensity of your breath. If you find your mind starts wandering, go back to focus on your stomach.

---

19 Sandra Bhandari, 'Meditation and yoga for ADHD', WebMD (17 January 2020), www.webmd.com/add-adhd/adhd-mindfulness-meditation-yoga, accessed 20 March 2021

20 Kate Kelly and Peggy Ramundo, 'Forget the lotus position: How to meditate ADHD style', ADDitude: Inside the ADHD mind, www.additudemag.com/how-to-meditate-for-adhd-symptoms, accessed 20 March 2021

5. Continue with this practice for up to three minutes to start. As you become more experienced, you can then try it for longer periods.

The emotional freedom technique

Another good way to reduce stress and anxiety is the emotional freedom technique (EFT) or 'tapping'. This is a holistic healing technique that has been proven to reduce stress and anxiety by up to 41%.[21] It involves tapping nine acupuncture pressure points while repeating positive messages. Professor Tony Stewart of Stratford University describes how tapping helps with depression, stress and anxiety; this technique can also be used by children.[22]

Tips for your wellbeing

Part of your role is to ensure others are aware and understand the challenges your child faces so you can help protect your child's interests. In a lot of cases, our children cannot communicate to others – teachers, doctors, friends – what they are feeling, and you have to do it for them. You are vital in their support system.

---

21 The Tapping Solution (no date) www.thetappingsolution.com, accessed 20 March 2021

22 Stewart, A, Boath, E, Carryer, A, Walton, I, & Hill, L, 'Can Emotional Freedom Techniques (EFT) be effective in the treatment of emotional conditions? Results of a service evaluation in Sandwell', *Journal of Psychological Therapies in Primary Care*, 2 (2013), 71–84.

To support your child effectively, you need to also look after yourself. Self-care is extremely important, as coping with a child with ADHD and/or related conditions can be exhausting. It's essential to stay positive and healthy yourself, as your behaviour has an influence on your child's emotional and physical health. Below are some tips for how to achieve this:

- **Maintain a positive attitude.** This is one of the hardest to achieve but keeping yourself calm and focused will help you establish and maintain good communications with your child.

- **Keep things in perspective.** Children with ADHD have difficulty regulating their behaviour without help and assistance; so what may seem extreme behaviour for their peers may be within the usual spectrum of behaviour for them. Having a sense of humour will also help.

- **Pick your battles and be open to compromise.** Celebrate the successes and make sure your expectations for your child are achievable.

- **Develop a support network.** You don't have to be alone. Talk to your child's doctor, therapists and teachers. Join an organisation or support group for parents. These are safe spaces for you to share your thoughts and experiences.

- **Accept offers of help so that you get a break.** Ensure that whoever is looking after your child is fully briefed and aware of how to cope so that you can switch off and not worry.

- **Find opportunities to reduce your stress levels.** A bubble bath in the evening, meditating in the morning and eating well will help to keep your stress levels down.

4
Acknowledge And Acceptance

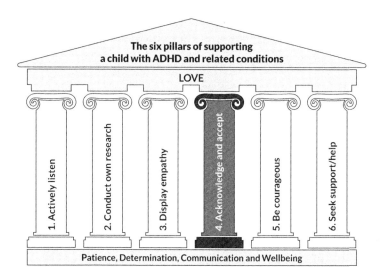

The six pillars of supporting
a child with ADHD and related conditions

LOVE

1. Actively listen

2. Conduct own research

3. Display empathy

4. Acknowledge and accept

5. Be courageous

6. Seek support/help

Patience, Determination, Communication and Wellbeing

The realisation that your child has a developmental or behavioural condition is a hard thing for any parent to accept. In some circumstances, it is obvious and visible. With children who have ADHD and/or related conditions, their challenges are mostly hidden and often unseen – even if the symptoms, such as a meltdown, are visible.

Figure 4.1, the image of an iceberg illustrates, above the water, the typical behaviours that we see in someone with ADHD. Below the surface, there are many other things going on that are often not seen.

It is not uncommon for parents to disagree about whether their child has a problem. I know of a number of cases where relationships have broken down because one parent cannot accept that their child has a learning challenge.

The vast majority of women I have spoken to who have a child with ADHD have said their husbands or partners did not believe their child had a developmental disorder and refused to attend meetings or discuss any support options. When my daughter first told me about Mekhi's developmental disorder, I don't think I really heard what she was saying. She mentioned his forgetfulness, that he was always losing things and falling over. Having had four children myself, I considered some of the behaviours she was describing to be typical, especially for boys. Yet for

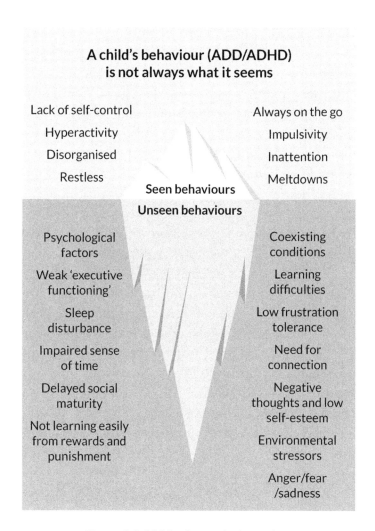

Figure 4.1 Hidden beneath the surface

Mekhi, these occurrences were almost daily. Though I didn't yet understand, Lynnette knew there was a problem.

Of course, as you've heard, I got there in the end, I reached the fourth pillar of the APD process – acknowledge and accept. I know that this acknowledgement and acceptance was key for my daughter. To have someone else understand what she was going through and the challenges she was facing on a daily basis was a huge relief. My acceptance also meant I was able to share my knowledge of Mekhi's condition with other family members, taking some of the burden away from Lynnette. Certain behaviours that we had all noticed made much more sense; what's more, we could all learn to help deal with them.

This journey has enabled me to acknowledge and accept my own parenting challenges, which has helped strengthen my relationship with my daughter. Whatever your story is, however you were brought up, whatever your lifestyle, your parenting approach has not caused ADHD or related conditions. These conditions will have an impact on your child's behaviour and the strategies you are able to use to manage this, but this is not because you are a bad person or parent. Do not beat yourself up. Do not waste time feeling guilty. You are working to improve the lives of your child and family; that is what counts.

Parenting a child with ADHD is difficult and requires courage, determination, planning, empathy and support. A child with ADHD processes information differently and needs different kinds of support. This is a long journey and progress may not come quickly.

You will require support and understanding from the people around you.

Practical ways to help your ADHD child

Your journey starts with acknowledging and accepting your child for who they are, recognising their strengths and understanding where they need your support. There are many practical steps you can take to make life easier at home. Often, these require some thinking ahead, as they typically involve organisation and planning, but once you get used to doing them, they should help to create and maintain a positive and healthy atmosphere at home. Remember, once you have found a format that works well with you and your child, share this with all the people your child regularly interacts with.

Organisation

- Creating routines will provide structure and help to avoid conflict. It's particularly important to have clear morning and evening routines. Consider where the challenges are for you and think about how you can build a routine around those tasks.

- Turn your routine into a visual, with a step-by-step guide using pictures and words, and then put this up somewhere your child can see it easily.

- Young children in particular will find rules useful, and this gives you easy phrases to use like, 'Remember the rule' or 'You know the rules'. With older children, you can agree the terms and use a rewards/consequences system.

- Predictability means your child will know what to expect, so be consistent in your approach. Carefully think through your rewards and sanctions and explain these to your child when you are both calm and collected. Explain whatever systems you are using to others your child has contact with, so they can apply them consistently.

- Reward good behaviour with immediate praise and deal with situations as soon as they arise.

Planning

- Break tasks down into small chunks and make them easily achievable by tackling one task at a time, for example, asking, 'Put your books away' rather than 'Tidy up your room'.

- Set short periods of time to complete tasks, for example thirty minutes for homework.

- Use visual reminders such as lists, tick sheets, diaries, alarms and timers.

- Be conscious of your child's particular needs, for example, if they are impulsive or have memory problems you may need to give them a reminder just before an event or situation, such as how to behave when in a shop.

- Pick your battles. Some things can be ignored; focus on the behaviour that absolutely needs to change.

- Plan ahead – you know when and where challenges are likely to occur, so be prepared.

Assistance

- Provide your child with help for as long as it is needed.

- Be specific when giving praise for an expected/ desired behaviour.

- Review and modify your reward system as it will need to be updated from time to time.

- It is important to show your child that you have heard them and that you have understood what they have said.

- Remind your child of their successes and times when they have demonstrated strength in a particular area.

- Share your knowledge about ADHD and your child's specific challenges with your family, friends and all the places your child attends, including out-of-school activities.

GIVING INSTRUCTIONS TO A CHILD WITH ADHD

Some children with ADHD struggle to process more than one instruction at a time or to understand what they are being asked to do. Because the ADHD brain is a little different in the way it processes things, we need to be extremely clear about what we want our child to do, so that they understand and can complete the task successfully.

The following are some tips that may help both you and your child manage their behaviours; these can be used by you and anyone else who looks after or has contact with your child, for example, a teacher.

- Get your child's attention before giving instructions, for example by touching their shoulder or arm (if touching is not an issue for them), saying their name and moving closer to them.

- If they're comfortable with direct eye contact, make eye contact so you can see that they are focused on what you are saying.

- Ensure the instruction is simple, clear and actionable, for example, 'Put the clothes from the floor into the wash basket' instead of, 'Tidy your bedroom'.

- Speak clearly and in a firm tone of voice.

- If you are not sure your child has understood your instruction, ask them to repeat it back to you in their own words.

- After giving the instruction, wait to see what they do. If they complete the task as requested, praise them immediately.

- If your child does not follow through with the instruction, use an 'if' and 'then' statement.

> For example, 'If you don't put the clothes from the floor in the wash basket right now, then you will lose time with your mobile phone today.' If they then complete the task, give them praise. If they do not complete the task, ensure you follow through with the threatened consequence.
>
> • Keep your approach consistent. Tell other people your child spends time with to give instructions in this way.

One of the things Mekhi had always wanted to do was learn to ride a bike. Lynnette knew this would be a challenge, so she bought him a bike with stabilisers. She knew how desperate he was to ride his bike unaided and, when she felt he was ready, she took Mekhi and his little brother to a huge park near where they lived for three weekends in a row. She coached him relentlessly, giving him the confidence to speed off down the track on his own, with no stabilisers. He fell off on numerous occasions and there were lots of tears and a few tantrums.

When she sent me the video of him riding his bike confidently, stopping by himself and staying on the bike, with her voice in the background willing him on, I cried: tears of joy for him and for her. She acknowledged her son's disabilities and accepted that he would have challenges, however, never gave up on him. Always believing that with enough practice and encouragement he could achieve the things he desired. This is evidence that, once you have acknowledged and accepted your child's condition, your focus can shift to ways of overcoming the challenges they face. This is something I experienced with Mekhi myself.

As a qualified life coach for adults and a certified WISDOM Coach® for children, I often ran workshops for kids, and Mekhi would come along. He enjoyed the stories I used to help teach children life skills. In one particular series of workshops, the children were learning about how to deal with bullying and peer pressure. Mekhi started out the class sitting in his seat like all the other students. When it became clear that concentration and sitting still would be an issue, he became my helper standing at the flipchart and turning the pages. He held my puppet while I told the story. He helped to give out resources and would always enjoy the activity, which would be either colouring in or creating something fun. I had to ensure he was always attended to, kept occupied and listened to during the session, and then he was able to enjoy it. The other children, although older than him, got to know him and encouraged him to take part in the lesson. He would proudly show his picture or activity at the end and pose for photos. It was lovely to have him as part of the workshop.

At another coaching session, we were talking about respect and self-respect and the impact that our behaviour had on others. He listened closely to the story and afterwards, when we talked about receiving

'Hearts and Marks'[23] as consequences of our actions. This is an activity that I use with children in my coaching work and that Lynnette now uses with Mekhi.

Rewards and consequences

To teach Mekhi about actions and consequences, I applied the 'Hearts and Marks system' – a reward or consequences system from the Adventures in Wisdom programme.[24] These are the behaviours Mekhi displayed that day that earned him rewards or consequences:

- He played well with his little brother: Heart

- He said please and thank you: Heart

- He cleared the plates from the table: Heart

- He upset his older sister: Mark

- He refused to turn off his iPad for dinner: Mark

The next time he saw me, at least a week later, the first thing he said was, 'I have ten hearts.' I was stunned that he had remembered and thrilled that this system for managing his behaviour had continued to work at home and that we could continue to build on it. It was a huge win.

---

23 I am a certified WISDOM Coach® and use the Adventures in WISDOM for Coaching Kids
24 Adventures in Wisdom Inc, https://adventuresinwisdom.com, accessed 25 February 2021

The reason I mention our success with this system, aside from the hope that it might also be useful for others, is that it was only possible because I had fully acknowledged and accepted Mekhi for who he was: a cute and cheeky six-year-old boy with ADHD. Because I had an understanding of his condition and had learned how to manage his behaviour, I was able to find and create tools that we could use to help him. To this day, Mekhi will do whatever he can to collect as many hearts as possible.

Rather than simply remembering the number of hearts and marks, I've found that having something tangible that your child can look at helps to embed and reinforce the learning, particularly useful for young children. One idea is to cut out physical shapes, such as a star and a moon shape, for example, that you can put into a small jar or box when they are earned and count up at the end of the day or week to determine the reward.

In addition to having a system for rewarding good behaviour and showing that there are consequences for poor behaviour, Lynnette did lots of research into activities that would suit Mekhi and found martial arts. It has discipline, routine and a level of complexity that activates the basal ganglia area of his brain (see Figure 3.1 in Chapter 3), which regulates communication between the body and the brain. This area is also responsible for motor control, facilitating movement and inhibiting competing movements. Martial arts also requires Mekhi to use his prefrontal cortex, the area responsible for organisation, cognitive flexibility, self-control and maintaining attention (again, see Figure 3.1).

At his first martial arts competition, Mekhi was one of the only children not to receive a prize. He was understandably emotional, but because of his ADHD his reaction was more extreme than would typically be expected. He ran over to his mum and cried loudly; the other parents were looking and commenting. It was a difficult moment. Lynnette felt upset for him and was in two minds about whether to put him forward for a competition again. But because of the positive impact martial arts was having on his development, and because he wanted to do it, she allowed him to enter again. The next competition came around and this time he received an award for most-improved student. He was overjoyed and so proud of himself.

This may seem like a small thing, and a neurotypical child might not consider it a big achievement, but for a child with ADHD or related condition these seemingly small wins are huge achievements that contribute to increasing their capabilities and self-confidence. With a mother who showed grit and determination to see her son succeed, Mekhi was moving forward and overcoming challenges.

I want to be extra clear here. Mekhi still has ADHD and other related conditions and he still struggles every day. When I pick him up from school, he nearly always appears happy, but he rarely remembers what he did in school that day. We hold hands as we walk to the car and I encourage him to think and talk about his day. More often than not, he is most interested in discovering what snack I have bought for him to eat on the way home. Acknowledging and accepting your child's condition is an important part of the process. Once you come to terms with your situation, you can begin to seek out solutions and assistance to enable and empower your child to succeed.

Wider acceptance and support

Of course, your own acknowledgement and acceptance is only one part of the picture, you will also need to consider your wider family and social network. As a result of your child's condition, plans you might have had may need to change. There may be an impact on your relationships, your work/career, your family dynamics and your social circle. As your network comes to learn about your situation, they will reach their own understanding, and either be supportive or not.

One of the members of our support group shared that her son's grandmother did not believe anything was wrong with her child. His grandmother thought that he was just a naughty child who needed to be disciplined. This is a common attitude among those who choose not to learn more about ADHD and other similar conditions. There will be others who know and understand more. You may even discover that there are people you know in similar situations. Lynnette has developed a good support network, including members of our family. Her siblings are particularly supportive, and our parents support network has provided a great source of encouragement. By connecting with others, you will undoubtedly hear their stories, which may be similar or completely different to your own. Below, I've shared with you a story I was told by another parent, Jane, about her daughter, Lydia.

LYDIA'S STORY

In my professional life, I have talked to many parents. One story that has stayed with me is that of Jane and her daughter, Lydia.

Jane and her husband quickly realised that Lydia was a special little girl. Though lacking a formal diagnosis, Jane believed that her daughter was on the autistic spectrum; she was bright yet quiet and reserved, especially in the company of people she didn't know well. She never got excited and rarely smiled. Jane was often told by other parents that Lydia was a rude child. Jane knew this was not the case.

When Lydia was seven years old, she had a huge tantrum after being told she could not attend her best friend's birthday party because she had misbehaved. She shouted at her mum, 'I hate you; I hate you.' Jane was so upset that she went and curled up into a ball on her bed, contemplating what to do. This had been Lydia's first tantrum and was the first confirmation that something was not right. A little while later, Jane noticed a presence in her bedroom. Lydia had quietly entered and was standing by the bed. Softly, she said, 'I'm sorry.'

Lydia's older sister suffered with obsessive compulsive disorder (OCD) and would clean the house three times a day. She also had a number of other medical conditions, and Jane was concerned that, as OCD is hereditary, Lydia might have similar issues at some time. As Lydia got older, she did indeed show some OCD traits. She liked to put things in order, and everything had its place. She found it difficult to communicate effectively and when asked a question would shrug her shoulders.

At school, Lydia was mostly well behaved. The teachers said she was so quiet they almost forgot she was in class. She was average in all subjects except art and cookery, in which she excelled. Jane encouraged her cooking and Lydia entered a competition. Even though she did not win, she did well, and Jane explained to her that this sometimes happened in life and helped her move past it. Lydia was also a talented artist but gave it up after a teacher discouraged her painstaking approach.

Once, at school, the parents of another child accused Lydia of trying to hurt their daughter; Lydia did not protest this accusation or make a scene. In fact, she had not tried to hurt the girl at all, the girl had hurt herself.

Jane described Lydia as being 'a quiet handful'. She was stubborn, liked to stay indoors and enjoyed time on the computer. She didn't smile or show excitement. She never spoke up for herself if she was wrongly accused of something, she always took the blame.

When Lydia was thirteen, she was bullied at school by a particular girl for many weeks. Most of the time she took the bullying. Then one day the girl pushed Lydia over. Being pushed – physically touched – changed things. Lydia retaliated. She had ripped the other girl's clothes – the incident had made her so angry. Lydia was sent home. Interestingly Lydia and the girl became the best of friends after this event.

Lydia had her first child when she was in her early twenties. Sadly, she was the victim of an abusive relationship. Similar to how she had been as a child, she never cried or told anyone about what was going on. She did not understand her partner's violent behaviour.

Jane always sought to protect her daughter. It was around this time that Lydia self-diagnosed her OCD. After this, when she had outbursts Jane would tell her that her behaviour was not normal but that, 'No matter what you do, it will not stop me loving you.' Lydia broke down in tears when she first heard this; she had needed to hear that she was loved.

Lydia was never medicated nor given any specific treatment. She now lives happily with her new partner and children and continues to use her cooking skills.

I asked Jane what advice she would give to other parents of a child with an anxiety or neurological development disorder. Here are her suggestions:

- Seek professional help and have your child assessed
- Show compassion and understanding – try not to judge your child based on their actions
- Pick your battles

- Try to understand that your child may find things more frightening than their peers
- Show your child you have their back
- Make sure your child knows you accept them for who they are and you love them

---

Tips for managing ADHD behaviours

Once Lynnette had acknowledged and accepted Mekhi's diagnosis and the implications of his conditions, she was able to shift her focus to establishing coping strategies. She has tried many approaches and techniques. Below, I've compiled some of the things she's found work best for them – remember, every child is different, so if not all of these work for you, don't worry. You're also bound to collect some tips of your own as you navigate your ADHD journey.

- **Getting dressed:** Mekhi is very competitive, so Lynnette turned getting dressed into a race. He loved the idea of trying to beat her to getting dressed in the morning. He didn't always end up fully dressed with everything in the right place or right way round, but every morning he was motivated to try. This approach also reduced the number of tantrums and outbursts that occurred first thing in the morning.

  Losing clothes at school: Mekhi was often losing bits of clothing at school, especially after

ACKNOWLEDGE AND ACCEPTANCE

PE. Lynnette created a laminated list of the items in his bag with a picture next to each item and would send this to school with him. He could then look at the pictures and make sure everything on the list was in the bag.

Lynnette also put name labels in all Mekhi's clothes, and let him design the labels. His favourite colour is red, and he loves football, so he designed a red label with a football on it. Lynnette showed him where the label was on all his clothing and where it should be against his body; because he had designed the label, he knew what to look for.

- **Eating too quickly:** Mekhi eats quickly, which can create a choking hazard. Before Lynnette learned how to deal with this behaviour, he struggled to regulate how much food he put in his mouth or consider the temperature of food before putting it in his mouth. He would stuff his mouth full of food even when it was piping hot. Lynnette has overcome this by:

  - Giving him small portions of food, letting him ask for more if he wants it.

  - Ensuring food is at a suitable temperature so that he can eat it straightaway.

  - Turning mealtimes into a game – who can chew their food five times, then ten times before swallowing – to help slow down his eating.

- Sitting next to him at the table so she can monitor him closely.

- Talking about the food they're eating, asking questions about what foods he likes, how the food is cooked. This also helps to slow down his eating.

- **Coping with meltdowns:** When Mekhi gets upset, he can be inconsolable. Using a 'time out' or 'the naughty step' just makes him angrier. He feels as if he is being ignored or that he is not wanted. If Lynnette can see that he is getting angry, she talks him through a breathing exercise: 'Breathe in for one, two, three, breathe out for one, two, three. This usually helps him regain calm. Reading a story is another way to calm him down. He loves being read to and has a special book that they turn to. Both these techniques work and give Lynnette an indication of how bad the meltdown is.

  Sometimes, distraction can snap him out of it. Lynnette will say she is going off to do something else and ask if he wants to help out. On occasions, she just lets him be angry, as long as he is in a safe place. This is usually his bedroom, which has nothing hanging from the walls or anything he could hurt himself with.

  If your child has been diagnosed with ADHD, the following tips may help if they are having a meltdown:

- Position yourself so that you are at eye level with your child. This will show them that you are on their side and want to hear what they have to say.

- Stay calm, don't show your anger and keep the attention on the two of you.

- When a child is screaming, lower your voice. Try to identify to your child what you think might be upsetting them: 'I know you are upset at the way I spoke to you…'

You will eventually understand what type of occurrence causes your child to have a meltdown, meaning it may be possible to avoid a tantrum before it starts. Practise different ways of getting through to your child in environments you are familiar with. This will help you and your child know what to expect.

Many children have conditions that affect their learning, development and behaviour, and these can manifest in different ways. None of this is your fault. When you and those around you are able to accept and acknowledge who they are, what challenges they face and what they enjoy, you will be better equipped to move forward, to seek out appropriate support and solutions, and help your child thrive.

5
Be Courageous

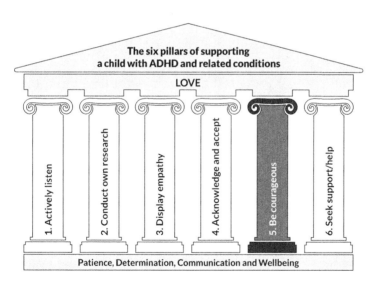

The six pillars of supporting
a child with ADHD and related conditions

LOVE

1. Actively listen

2. Conduct own research

3. Display empathy

4. Acknowledge and accept

5. Be courageous

6. Seek support/help

Patience, Determination, Communication and Wellbeing

Acourageous person faces up to danger and fights against the odds. Courage is the ability to take on difficulties and pain, despite fear. Courage is more than a quality of character, it is a state of mind, and it is one of the most important pillars in the APD process. All adults and parents need to have courage, but for a parent of a child or children with special educational needs and neurodiverse needs, a different level of courage is required.

Many of the parents I have spoken to about their experiences mention the 'fight' they have had to get the support they needed for their child or children. To be an effective advocate for your child, you need to have courage. I talked to an American parent of four children, all with ADHD; she had also been diagnosed with ADHD herself. She described this constant fight for support. Although her oldest child was twenty-one years old, she still needed to fight to get him the support he needed.

The courage to fight on

It is common for parents to be suffering with their own mental health conditions; often, they feel close to falling apart. This is why a good support network is critical. When Lynnette feels particularly under pressure, I am able to support her and lift her spirits. If you can't get this from family and friends, being part of a support group will help you to know you are not alone and give you the courage to keep going.

In the UK, there is a rising number of cases of local authorities being taken to court to appeal decisions against granting an EHCP.[25,26] As a result, support groups have popped up in different areas as parents have nowhere else to go. Talking to other parents and carers in a similar position is the only support some people have.

Families with children who have special educational needs can be severely disrupted. Those parents with careers are challenged, finances can suffer due to additional costs and relationships can be put under strain. More often than not, the process of having a child assessed and/or diagnosed is a struggle. You may then have a similar fight to get the school to put necessary interventions in place. As a parent, you might start to question your own judgement. This whole process can take a toll on one's mental health.

From a financial perspective, it can be very costly for parents to get the appropriate support in education for their child: purchasing educational aids to help at home and in the classroom. Then there is paying

25 Matt Keer, 'The latest SEND tribunal figures paint a troubling picture', *special needs jungle* (18 June 2019), www.specialneedsjungle. com/latest-send-tribunal-figures-paint-a-troubling-picture, accessed 20 March 2021

26 *The Good School Guide*, 'Refusal to assess for an EHCP' (no date), www.goodschoolsguide.co.uk/special-educational-needs/legal/ refusal-to-assess-for-an-ehcp, accessed 20 March 2021

out for private appointments with a child psychologist and speech therapist if they can afford to go that route.

Lynnette's eldest daughter suffered with anxiety in her teens; her younger daughter has had challenges at secondary school and is being assessed for dyslexia. Her youngest son is showing signs of ADHD. Having a family where all your children require support for additional needs and are demanding your attention in some way is a challenge for any parent.

The parent of a child with learning difficulties and neurodiverse behaviour is a unique kind of person. I believe these people were chosen for this role because of the type of person they are: caring, thoughtful, kind, willing to go the extra mile, supportive, empathetic and courageous. Some parents don't realise they have these special qualities until they are pointed out by someone else. Don't get me wrong, they still get stressed, have days they wish things were different, wonder why this is happening to them, feel depressed and get anxious, but they are always there as an advocate for their child. It can sometimes take the parent/carer a while to get there, but it becomes their mission.

In the following sections, I've provided some information that should help equip you in your fight for support, so that you know what you are entitled to, how and where you can get it, and what the process is likely to be like. Hopefully, this will help give you the courage to continue fighting.

Push for progress

Earlier in the book, we talked about the EHCP – the legal document granted and produced by the local authority setting out a child's special educational needs and the extra support they will require.

Once they have received a request for an EHCP, the local authority typically has six weeks to decide whether or not to carry out an EHC assessment. In my research, I have found that there is disparity among UK councils in the way they manage the EHC assessment process. Depending on where you live, the time frame and quality of the EHC assessment and plan can vary, and there may be gaps in the plan and delays in getting it. The number of children requiring special education is rising. In January 2020, there was an increase of 10% on the previous year of EHC plans maintained by local authorities in the UK.[27] As a parent or carer of a child with special educational needs you need to have courage, grit, determination and be prepared for a fight to obtain the support your child needs. Once you get an EHCP, the battle is not

---

27 *Education, health and care plans* (Gov.UK Statistics, 7 May 2020), https://explore-education-statistics.service.gov.uk/find-statistics/ education-health-and-care-plans, accessed 20 March 2021

THE ADHD SUPPORT HANDBOOK

over; you then need to monitor its implementation and keep pushing for progress updates.

EHCP SIX-MONTH REVIEW

I saw first-hand with Lynnette and Mekhi that getting an EHCP in place is not the end of the road. Six months on from the EHCP being granted, Lynnette was not happy with many things that had occurred and had a lot of questions she wanted answered. Together, we conducted research, re-read notes and letters from professionals and planned her approach to the six-month EHCP assessment for Mekhi with his school. At this time, she gained much inspiration and guidance from her support system, which helped her maintain a positive attitude and outlook.

Lynnette knew that this meeting would determine the level of support Mekhi would have going forward. It was vital that she was able to present the information she had collected in a coherent, structured and confident way so that she was taken seriously. One of the key things she did not want to happen was to fall apart in the meeting and not be able to communicate what she needed to. She printed her list of questions along with the research she had done in relation to statements made in the EHCP. She was able to professionally challenge the school and council officers, giving evidence and asking appropriate questions which they should have had the answers for but did not. The meeting was two-and-a-half hours long. Lynnette's husband was impressed by the way she handled the meeting.

Fortunately, the special educational needs coordinator (SENCo) was supportive and suggested that another referral to a speech and language occupational therapist for reassessment was appropriate. The meeting ended with a plan of action with clear timelines for following up. Lynnette knew she would have to chase up those actions and continue to ensure Mekhi received the support he needed. The fight continued!

Finding the courage to calmly and professionally challenge and question your child's school and/or the local authority is not an easy task. Ultimately, parents and carers are the only ones who know their child and understand the impact a lack of support will have on their lives.

Your child's advocate

To help you in your own fight for support for your child in school, I've included some of the questions, concerns and observations Lynnette prepared ahead of Mekhi's EHCP review. These issues are specific to Mekhi, but will give you an idea of the types of questions to ask and things to highlight, which you can use as a guide and adapt to your child/circumstances as appropriate:

- Out of the twenty-five hours of support suggested in Mekhi's EHCP, how many of those hours are currently in one-to-one support?

- How will the support recommended in the EHCP be implemented and managed?

- How is funding used for Mekhi?

- Does Mekhi's one-to-one support person have experience of his challenges? What training in ADHD, dyspraxia and developmental delay have they had? How successful have they been with previous children they have supported, particularly those with similar conditions?

- The support Mekhi is current receiving for his vocabulary is not benefitting his speech, how can this be improved?

- What handwriting support is Mekhi receiving?

- How is Mekhi redirected in class when he is not paying attention?

- How often does Mekhi have an outburst in class and how is this managed?

- What assessments are being used in the school to assess his progress since the implementation of the EHCP? How long have these assessments been used in the school and what outcomes have they had?

- How is Mekhi's progress being measured against the national curriculum?

- I have been told that Mekhi is still performing below the level expected, what will happen at the end of Key Stage 2 to close his achievement gap?

- How can you determine the level Mekhi is working at, and is he being taught at this level?

- What targets are being set for Mekhi in class?

- The work that he is being asked to do with his current support is not appropriate, due to his conditions, and his academic skills need to be improved. How can this be adjusted to his skills level? Mekhi wants to learn but needs the support to do so.

- Why is Mekhi's work on the ELSA programme not being measured? (ELSA stands for emotional literacy support assistant. This consists of resources to teach emotional literacy or EI to children). If Mekhi is not progressing using this programme, is this wasting time?

- What is a Sandwell's assessment, and how is it being used?

- What are the criteria for accessing the resource centre attached to the school?

- What other support provisions are available in the county?

During the review, Lynnette praised the assistance provided by the school but voiced her concerns about the way the EHCP was being implemented and about

Mekhi's academic development, with a view to working with the school not against them. It is helpful to build and maintain a good relationship with the school and SENCo, but courage is still required to ensure the support your child needs is implemented effectively, giving them the best chance of academic success.

It is imperative that when you go into these meetings you are well prepared. You need to have done your homework and be able to speak the language of the professionals you're meeting. Keep all the paperwork, letters, emails and any correspondence related to your child so that you can refer back to this as needed.

Find the courage to advocate for your child. Challenge and question. Don't be afraid of seeming 'pushy'. Sometimes, you have to be strong rather than liked. The school and SENCo will have hundreds of children demanding their attention; you have to be the one fighting their corner. One parent who faced a particularly hard battle was Sarah, who told me about the challenges she faced in advocating for her son, James.

JAMES' STORY

James was labelled as a 'naughty boy' from a young age. His mother, Sarah, was frequently called in to nursery, and later school, because of his behaviour. She knew that his behaviour was not 'normal' but would not have described it as naughty.

As James progressed through primary school, the amount of time the learning support assistant was assigned to him increased. James' parents tried to get him an EHC assessment, but the head teacher said it would affect the school's position in the league tables and that they did not know what they were doing in suggesting this approach. When James moved up to secondary school, it was expected that the level of learning support he was receiving would decrease. In fact, it was the opposite – though he was not considered to be in need of a teaching assistant (TA) or EHCP. He became depressed and his parents were heartbroken to see their twelve-year-old so unhappy.

An educational assessment had been carried out by the local authority, but each time James did the test, the result differed considerably. This was not useful to his parents and they decided to pay for a private full educational assessment, which was damning of the school. James was diagnosed with severe dyslexia, dyspraxia and a very short memory span; there was also an issue with his eyes. He had a high IQ, but at the age of eleven he had a reading age of four.

The private assessor referred James to a London ophthalmic hospital for extensive tests, which revealed that James lived in a green world: he could only see green. Colour blindness ran in Sarah's family, but not this severe. James was referred to an optician who specialised in dyslexia and prescribed yellow tinted glasses.

On receiving the report, the educational assessor suggested that James could be labelled as 'disabled'. To support James' development, his parents enrolled him in a private after-school programme. Within weeks, his reading age improved from age four to age thirteen. He asked to read *The Hobbit*. The educational assessor explained that, because James had struggled in class to read from the whiteboard, he had given up. He couldn't see it properly and couldn't write enough down before the teacher wiped it off.

James is now twenty-nine and runs a successful business. He was helped to understand his needs and has developed ways to manage them. For example, he takes notes, as his short-term memory is still a challenge.

I asked Sarah what her top tips would be to other parents of children experiencing challenges; she said:

- Don't give up – you know your child better than anyone
- Invest in a full assessment by a specialist if you can (GPs aren't specialists)
- Support your child as best you can as a parent, not as a specialist or therapist
- Don't beat yourself up, there is help out there

James' story highlights the challenges that parents can face, and the courage required to seek appropriate support.

Not all families can invest in a private assessment, but as parents you can continue to challenge the school and local authority until you feel you are being heard. Keeping a record of impacts and behaviours will help. Sarah had the courage to keep looking for alternative ways to support her son and, as a result, he thrived.

Reaching for success

With your courage and support, you can help your child thrive, too. Don't be afraid to encourage your child to stretch themselves and set themselves ambitious goals. In the same way that your journey started with acknowledging and accepting your child for who they are, recognising their strengths and understanding where they need your support, so your journey continues. As before, there were many practical steps you could take to make life easier at home, so too are there steps you can take to help your child achieve their goals and reach their full potential.

Quick guide to goal setting

Good goals are **outcome focused.** Help your child understand what their strengths are and what it is they want to achieve, and, as with breaking down instructions, break the path to achieving their goals into manageable steps.

KEEP IT IN THE POSITIVE

Remember, goals should inspire you, not be something to beat yourself up with. So, help your child to frame their goal in the positive:

To achieve them, goals should be SMART:

- **S**pecific (so you know exactly what you're trying to achieve)
- **M**easurable (so you know when you've achieved it)
- **A**ction-oriented (so you can do something about it)
- **R**ealistic (so it is achievable)
- **T**ime-bound (so you have a deadline)

Help your child think about the size of their goals, and whether they are too small or too big. Too big? Break down into smaller goals. Too small? Incorporate it as a step towards a larger goal. A good idea is to set a goal with a range, so your child can't fail to achieve. What would be the minimum, easy-to-achieve level of a particular goal, and what would be the maximum target level to reach? What would be an extraordinary level of that goal to achieve?

You could use the chart below (Figure 5.1) to help your child create focus and feel motivated towards achieving their goals.

I have also created a workbook that outlines seven steps to goal setting here: https://activepersonal development.co.uk/adhd-support-handbook-resources (check back to the Introduction for the password).

My Plan of Action   Date: ....

Goal: ....
....

Task	Start Date	Finish Date	Status	Notes

Figure 5.1 My plan of action form

Creating a vision board

Something that can help children with ADHD – and their families – with goal setting and motivation, is a vision board. This is a collection of a wide variety of inspirational collages created from pictures and a powerful way to make your dreams feel more tangible and attainable. The very act of creating the vision board tells your mind what is important and what you want to focus on in your life.

A vision board can be used to help set goals for the year (or other time period) ahead. It could also focus on a specific area like school, home life, friendships, activities and interests. For your child, you might focus on a particular skill or strength and find pictures and words that help them to visualise what they are working towards. It may be that your child wants to become a football player or a policeman when they grow up. Find pictures and words that relate to these roles. What skills will they need to develop? How do they need to behave? Find pictures of footballers they admire, or policemen in uniform.

A VISION BOARD FOR MEKHI

When he was seven, we helped Mekhi to create his vision board and asked him questions including:

- What do you want to do when you grow up?
- Who do you want to be like?
- What do you want things to be like at school?
- What activities do you want to learn?
- What do you want your family to be like?
- What is your favourite colour?
- What positive things will you say to yourself?
- How do you want to feel?
- What sports do you want to play?

We found pictures and words to represent his answers and created his vision board. Before we did this, we'd had no idea he was interested in the police force – it's amazing what you can learn about your child.

CREATING A VISION BOARD

You will need:

- A large blank piece of card stock, A3 or larger, or a computer application such as PowerPoint or Word.

- If you're using paper, you'll need colourful felt-tip pens, a pair of scissors and glue sticks.

- A supply of colourful, beautiful, inspirational magazines. You can also use the internet to find images.

Getting started

With a vision board, how you feel is more important than what you think. While they look for pictures, encourage your child to let their mind run free. Make the board vibrant and dynamic. Cut out anything that inspires a positive or curious response from your child; don't analyse, just go for it. You should include pictures, symbols, words and quotes, anything that resonates with or appeals to them. It doesn't need to make sense, follow a theme, or be obvious why they're drawn to it. The aim is to create something inspiring and personal.

Once you've finished

When you've finished creating your child's vision board, put it somewhere they will see it every day to remind, inspire and focus them. Sometimes, when we

see something regularly, after a while we stop noticing it, so once in a while encourage them to sit or stand
and really look at it. Encourage them to feel it and get
excited by it. Just before bedtime is a great time to do
this, as they can ponder and absorb it overnight. You
can also use it to help your child set small goals that
will help them move towards their vision.

Tips for maintaining your mental health

Being courageous and fighting to be the best advocate for your child can take its toll if you don't look
after yourself, so it's important that you protect your
mental and physical health. Below are a few tips to
consider:

- **Believe in yourself.** As a parent/carer you know
  what your child needs – follow your intuition.

- **Eat well.** Your physical health and wellbeing
  affect your mental health and wellbeing; it's
  important to look after both.

- **Exercise.** Keeping physically fit will help you
  maintain a positive attitude, as well as increase
  your physical capabilities. The chemical reactions that take place following exercise help
  to reduce anxiety and stress and will improve
  your mood. Research has shown that chemicals
  produced in the brain through exercise help to

reduce the symptoms of ADHD.[28] If you already have a regular exercise routine in place and are physically fit, it will be easier to introduce exercise for you and your child.

- **Manage stress.** There are many different techniques that can help you relax and find a sense of calm, such as meditation and yoga.

- **Be present.** Focus on the now, rather than past or future events.

- **Develop a good sleep routine.** Lack of sleep can negatively impact your mental health.

- **Build good personal relationships** at home, work and in your community. This is important to your mental health and will ensure you have a solid support network.

- **Make time for fun.** Laughter releases stress, boosts morale and lifts your mood.

- **Seek help** if you need it. There is no shame in asking for help when you need it. It takes courage to seek help, but it can change your life.

When something in particular is causing you to feel stressed, try the following:

---

28   Claudia Verret, Marie-Claude Guay, Claude Berthiaume, Phillip Gardiner and Louise Beliveau, 'A physical activity program improves behavior and cognitive functions in children with ADHD: An exploratory study', *Journal of Attention Disorders*, 16/1 (13 September 2010), 71–80, https://journals.sagepub.com/doi/abs/10.1177/1087054710379735, accessed 21 March 2021

- Notice when you feel stressed and try to identify what situations or events impact you the most.

- Work through finding a solution; this will make the problem easier to face.

- Talk through your problem with a trusted friend; expressing how you are feeling will unburden you and help to reduce the stress. Consult a professional if needed.

- Read books or consult a health professional to help with de-stressing techniques.

- If work is a stressor, consult your superior or colleagues to find strategies you can put in place to help you.

- Practise delegation, where possible, and be clear on priorities.

- Don't beat yourself up.

6

Seek Support And Help

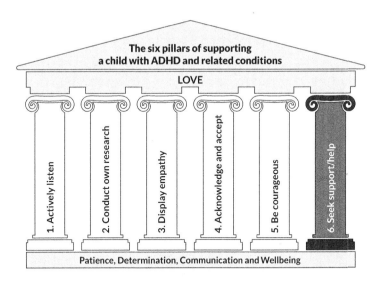

The six pillars of supporting
a child with ADHD and related conditions

LOVE

1. Actively listen

2. Conduct own research

3. Display empathy

4. Acknowledge and accept

5. Be courageous

6. Seek support/help

Patience, Determination, Communication and Wellbeing

We have reached the last pillar, but this is not the end of the story. For you, as a parent or carer, it is likely only the beginning.

First, you must remember *you are not alone*. Many parents are facing the same or similar challenges to you. There is support out there, you just have to look for it. I recommend seeking out a support group, online or in person. You could start with the Facebook group I have established, The ADHD Revolution (www.facebook.com/groups/theadhdrevolution), where you will find free resources, tools and information along with a growing community aiming to change the ADHD story.

This chapter is intended to give you some practical advice and resources that may make life easier for you and your child. In that spirit, before we get stuck into the practical advice and resources, I've put together an action plan outlining the steps you can start taking today for an easier tomorrow.

Action plan

This action plan will help you take the next steps on your journey to supporting your child and yourself. Take a moment to consider which actions, if any, you want to take:

- **Who can I talk to?** Build a support network of family, friends and professionals you can talk to and who can help when you are feeling low.

- **Benefits and entitlements:** Check to see what financial support you are entitled to in your local authority.

- **The ADHD profile:** Take control. Generate an ADHD profile of your child and their specific needs with the help of your child's GP and teacher.

- **Talk to the teacher:** Enlist the help of your child's teacher to identify and implement practical steps that can help with your child's specific needs and their day-to-day learning.

- **Supporting changes and transitions:** Enlist the help of professionals as your child grows and changes and progresses through the education system.

- **The support of a coach:** As your needs and those of your child change, look for additional support systems.

In the following pages you will find an array of information that will help you gain a deeper understanding of ADHD and related conditions, and links to books and resources that will assist you on your journey.

Who can I talk to?

There were times when my daughter didn't know who to talk to. Even when she did have someone around, she still felt alone and unable to discuss her son's condition. My role as Lynnette's mother has been as a sounding board for her concerns. We talk through what is happening and discuss how best to move forward. She also shares her successes with me and the ongoing challenges she faces. Having a support system is key to helping her to maintain her wellbeing. Parents in her position are constantly fighting to get their children the support required. It is an ongoing battle, but you need not fight it alone.

Sometimes, you simply need a shoulder to cry on, someone to turn to for emotional support, but sometimes you will need professional guidance and advice. It's important to know that there is help and support out there, whether you prefer to connect online, or in person. I've listed some starting points for you below:

- **Your GP:** They can refer your child to specialists for assessment.

- **Child and Adolescent Mental Health Service (CAMHS):** An NHS service that assesses and treats young people with emotional, behavioural and mental health difficulties. Referrals through your GP, school or social worker.

- **Paediatrician:** Conducts assessments to confirm diagnosis and provide ongoing support.

- **Class teacher:** Advises on behaviour in class setting; implements recommendations for support in school.

- **SENCo:** Usually located in your child's school or may be associated with a number of schools in your area.

- **Headteacher:** Supports class teacher's recommendations and implements school support.

- **Health visitor and/or social worker:** Helps identify development problems and assists families in getting help at an early stage.

- **Educational psychologist:** Conducts assessment and confirms diagnosis.

- **Local council:** Information and guidance on the resources available in your area.

- **ADHD organisations:** Information, guidance and resources (www.adhdfoundation.org.uk and www.chadd.org).

- **YoungMinds:** Free, confidential online/telephone support for parents and young people https://youngminds.org.uk.

- **The ADHD Revolution:** Facebook group of people living with ADHD who want to change the story about ADHD, gain or give support www.facebook.com/groups/theadhdrevolution.

Please note that I do not endorse any particular organisation and you should do your own due diligence and research.

Your GP

Visiting your GP to discuss your child's behaviour is usually the first step of your journey; you may be referred to your GP by the school. It is important that you go prepared so that you can ensure you obtain all the necessary information, and your GP gets the full picture of your situation. Below are some tips for how to prepare and what to think about before you go:

Booking an appointment

- Ask for a GP who has experience of your child's condition or is used to dealing with children with neurodiverse conditions

- Request the earliest appointment of the day, you may not have to wait as long

- If you don't want to be rushed, request the latest appointment of the day

Things to take to the appointment

- Any notes that you have made when observing your child's behaviour or condition, for example, a symptom diary

- Any letters or reports you have received from the school that detail your child's behaviour there

- Information about any comorbid condition/s you suspect your child may have that you have gathered through research, and any questions you have about it/them

- A friend or relative for support

At the appointment

- Tell the GP you think your child has a problem, give this problem a name if you know or suspect it, for example, ADHD or dyslexia

- Explain why you think your child has this condition and give up to five examples of symptoms they have displayed

- Using the information you have researched, link this back to your evidence and your child's behaviour

- Talk to your GP about the conversations you have had with the school, if you were referred by them

- Ensure the GP reviews all the information you have taken with you and, in particular, correspondence between you and the school

- If your child has been displaying symptoms for more than six months, needs support at school and you have evidence to support your concerns, ask your GP for a formal full diagnostic assessment for ADHD (or other conditions)

If your GP won't refer

- Ask them to explain why they do not want to refer your child and write down what they say

- Inform the GP that you know that the NHS Act 2006, the Care Act 2014 and the Children and Families Act 2014 provide a statutory framework for supporting people with special educational needs or a disability

- Get a second opinion: book an appointment with another GP

- If you continue to have your requests refused, consider changing your surgery or, in extreme circumstances, seek legal advice

Medication

You may want to speak to your GP or paediatrician to discuss whether medication is an appropriate route to take with your child. In certain circumstances, medication can make life easier for children and young people with ADHD – helping to improve attention, concentration and enabling them to process information more efficiently or communicate better.

Benefits and entitlements

As we touched on in Chapter 5, families with children who have special educational needs can face financial as well as emotional challenges. Getting appropriate assessment and support can incur costs, but there are benefits and support resources available in England – a summary of which is provided on my website (https://activepersonaldevelopment. co.uk/adhd-support-handbook-resources. See the Introduction for the password.) You may need to contact your local authority to confirm availability and eligibility criteria in your area. The following are a few entitlements that you may find useful.

Name of entitlement	Contact
Disability Living Allowance – for a child under 16 years old requiring extra financial support.	www.gov.uk/ disability-living- allowance-children/ eligibility
Personal Independence Payment (PIP) – for anyone over 16 years old requiring extra financial support.	www.gov.uk/pip/ eligibility

Continued

Cont.

Name of entitlement	Contact
Educational Health Care Plan (EHCP) – a legal document that provides a child or young person with Special Educational Needs additional support while in an educational setting.	www.ipsea.org.uk/ ehc-needs-assessments
Max Card – available to families with additional needs providing free or discounted access to fun activities in the UK.	https://mymaxcard. co.uk
Hidden disabilities lanyard – this is a discreet way to alert people to the fact you or someone with you may need additional support, help or more time. Available in the UK, USA, NL, AUS, BEL, CAN and NZL.	https://hidden disabilitiesstore.com
CEA Card – enables people with disabilities who want to visit the cinema apply for a complimentary ticket for someone to go with them.	www.ceacard.co.uk

The ADHD Profile

Consistency for someone with neuro-behavioural difficulties is often key. It is important that all the people who will come into contact with your child have an understanding of your child's condition. The key information in your child's ADHD Profile will help them manage situations and adapt as necessary to ensure your child gets the support they need. It might be given to a new class teacher, a swimming instructor, therapist, childminder, or any other person your child regularly spends time with.

There is a template online that you can print or copy and use at your leisure (https://activepersonaldevelopment. co.uk/adhd-support-handbook-resources. See the Introduction for the password.) It is also included in the 'Useful websites' section at the end of this chapter and shown in Figure 6.1.

These profiles can make a huge a difference to children joining activities outside of the home. It means they are better understood and supported in a way that meets their needs.

Talk to the teacher

Once your child has been diagnosed with neuro-behavioural difficulties, talk to your child's teacher about reasonable adjustments that can be made in school. These are some suggestions of what may prove helpful for children with ADHD and keep them focused:

Avoiding distraction

- Position in classroom (away from window, door, back of class). Preferably at the front close to teacher
- Sit them next to a buddy/behaviour mentor

	This ADHD profile belongs to:	This is a photo of me:
ADHD is a neurodevelopmental condition. I think and process information differently.		
The information in this profile will help you to understand how to get the bets out of me and the challenges I face.	Overview statement:	
Impulsivity, hyperactivity and inattention are the main symptoms of my condition. You will find examples of what that means at the bottom of the page.	My strengths:	Things that I may find difficult:
I love praise, it helps me to know that I am doing things right.	Things that help me:	Notes/Action plans:
I dont have lots of friends so please look out for me at break times.		
Please be patient with me - I may have related conditions. I'm doing my very best.	Diagnosis/medication I'm on and how this may affect me:	Signed: _____ Parent/carer: _____

Impulsivity: Lacks self-control, difficulty taking turns, interrupts, talks back, loses temper

Hyperactivity: Can't sit still, fidgets, talks a lot, always on the go, restlessness

Inattention: Disorganised, doesn't follow through, doesn't pay attention, forgetfulness, loses things, late with homework

Figure 6.1 ADHD profile

- Provide adult support for less structured tasks

- Provide visual checklists

- Give regular rest or movement breaks

- Provide area of calm within class they can retreat to if necessary

- Fidgeter – keep hands busy

Support academic achievement

- Provide short single step instructions, so they are able to keep up and achieve

- Provide visual examples to model what is expected

- Provide a visual list of steps (to support the single step instructions)

- Break down tasks into small chunks, with a visual of end result

- Give them opportunities to show their strengths

- Give them opportunities to hold responsible positions ie prefect, book monitor

- Agree a secret communication to provide behaviour feedback eg thumbs up or down

Social and emotional wellbeing

- Ensure all staff they come into contact with have had ADHD training and are aware of the Equality Act

- Make structured activities available at break times

- Identify potential triggers and have an adult support available

- Have a calm space available in the classroom

- Provide a buddy role model to help them copy and apply positive behaviours

- Give visual timetables and checklists and agree a notification mechanism when change or transitions will happen

Supporting changes and transitions

Times of change and transitions can be challenging for most of us. Children with ADHD can find these times particularly stressful. As with all children, it's important to keep communication channels open so you can try to understand what they are thinking and what they want for their lives.

These are a few questions you could ask that will help you to understand how your child is feeling as they go through the transitions of life. You don't need to ask them all at once, perhaps over a few days or weeks, as a conversation starter:

- What is bothering you at the moment?

- What things do you want to achieve and when?

- What would you like to stop?

- What would you like to change about school/college/friendships/home?

- What are you fearful of?

- What, if anything, is important to keep the same?

These are open questions that should shed some light on what is going on in your child's life and what they aspire to achieve. Try to avoid asking 'why' questions, as they could become defensive and close down. If they tell you something you want to know more about, try following up with a less direct, 'Tell me more about it.' If they've mentioned something they want to change, ask when they would like that to happen; you could then work towards developing a short- or long-term plan of action to achieve the change they want. Focus on agreeing the one or two steps that will help move them forward.

Some children with ADHD will particularly struggle with the stresses that come with growing up and it will be necessary to thoroughly prepare them to deal with the transition from the safe confines of primary school to the often bigger and more overwhelming secondary school environment.

THE ADHD SUPPORT HANDBOOK

Transitioning between primary and secondary school

There are practical steps that you can take to help your child cope before your child transitions – professionals within the school can help and advise early in the process.

Most secondary schools have an integration programme, but your child might need a tailored approach to the upcoming change. You should discuss and agree this with both your child's current and new teacher. Something as simple as a video introducing the new teacher in advance of the start date will help your child begin the process of change. Typical issues that can arise in the transition from primary to secondary school are making new friends, forming relationships with new teachers and dealing with the size of the school.

Transitioning between secondary school and college/university

Young people with ADHD often struggle settling into new surroundings, and higher education will almost certainly involve new surroundings and new challenges. The first year in particular can be difficult. The college/university environment is quite different from the secondary school environment, and planning for this step up will help to reduce confusion and anxiety. A few topics to think about when transitioning from secondary school to higher education in the UK include:

Secondary school	College/university
Classes 6 hours a day/5 days a week	Number of classes will vary each week
20–30 students in class	30+ students in class/ lectures
Access to class teacher before or after school is easy	Tutor access may be restricted to certain times or via an assistant
Set schedule for classes with very few changes	Class times and days may vary
Small amounts of homework on a regular basis	Projects will be larger, with an increased amount of study time per day
Teachers check the homework completed	Tutors may not check students' work and self-directed learning expected
Students are reminded by teachers of work that has not been completed	Students may not be reminded by tutors of missing or late work
Teachers will approach students if they feel they need help	It is assumed students will ask for assistance if they need it

As before, anticipate the potential issues that could arise from the transition and enlist the help and support of the professionals at the institution your child hopes to attend.

The support of a coach

As your child grows into an adult, the support they need will obviously change, and so will the support that you need in order to support them to change and grow. Coaching can be a help to both parents and their children. There are many reasons why parents seek coaching support for themselves or for their child. Here are some of the most common:

- When there is conflict at home, either involving or in the presence of the child

- Dealing with low self-confidence and/or anxiety – of parent and/or child

- Loneliness – a child might have few friends and believes no one likes them; a parent feels isolated in dealing with the demands of raising a child with ADHD

- Behaviour challenges that disrupt family life, personal relationships, work

- Parents want help to know how to support their child and involve the child in learning techniques to help themselves

Coaching is a powerful and effective resource parents can tap into to support themselves and their family. With coaching, children can learn mindset skills that will help them deal with the ups and downs of growing up, particularly those children struggling with self-confidence, self-belief and self-esteem issues. Often, the behaviours displayed mask the way a child thinks about themselves. A coach will be able to determine quickly if a child or young person will benefit from a coaching programme after an initial conversation. Working with a coach can help children develop the skills, confidence and ability to thrive.

STATS AND FACTS

Did you know that:

- 30% of 'tweens' (children between the ages of ten and twelve) experience headaches and difficulty sleeping as a result of stress?[29]
- 25% of children between the ages of thirteen and eighteen suffer from anxiety disorders?[30]
- 10% of children are diagnosed with depression before the age of eighteen?[31]

29 A Fogel, *Is Your Child Stressed Out? Why You May Not Know*, *Psychology Today* (7 Jan 2010), www.psychologytoday.com/gb/blog/body-sense/201001/is-your-child-stressed-out-why-you-may-not-know, accessed 21 March 2021

30 National Institute of Mental Health, *Any Anxiety Disorder*, www.nimh.nih.gov/health/statistics/any-anxiety-disorder.shtml, accessed 21 March 2021

31 J Kluger, 'The Happiness of Pursuit', *Time* (8 July 2013), http://content.time.com/time/magazine/article/0,9171,2146449,00.html, accessed 19 April 2021

Tips for parents

Wherever you are on your ADHD journey, it is important to remember you are not alone. The following
tips will help you support yourself and your child.

1. It is OK to ask for help. The sooner you reach
   out and find support the better you will feel.
   The sighs and tears of relief I have seen when
   people find others who get it speaks volumes.

2. Your child's condition does not define who they
   are and who they will be. Look for strategies to
   help them manage the challenges they and you
   experience.

3. It is OK not to be OK.

4. Develop positive relationships with the people
   your child comes into contact with and share with
   them your child's strengths and challenges. This
   will help them to build strong relationships with
   your child providing a supportive network for
   them and you.

5. Your role is to help your child become
   independent. Nurture, support and teach them
   to take responsibility. Let them know you
   have their back. Understand their entitlements
   and the benefits available to support your child's
   educational and social development.

6. Focus on your child's strengths and praise their
   achievements.

Conclusion

Many children have conditions that affect their learning, development and behaviour, and these can manifest in many different ways. None of this is your fault. When you and those around you see that some things are different for your child, actively listen to find out what these differences are, accept and acknowledge who your child is, understand the challenges they face and learn how to support them courageously and whole-heartedly. You will be better equipped to forge a strong relationship with your child, seek out appropriate support and solutions, and help your child to thrive.

At the start of, and throughout, your journey, you will need to learn about ADHD and any other related or relevant conditions so that you fully understand your child's diagnosis, the challenges they face, and the impact these will have on your own life and that of your family. This will also enable you to 'speak the language' of the professionals you will be in contact with, and to ask for the support you need.

This will not be an easy journey. You will need to dig deep, be resilient and courageous, as you may have to fight to get your child the support they need. As such, it is critical that you look after your wellbeing so you can better care for your child.

Always remember that there is light at the end of the tunnel.

Your journey continues, and I hope that you will be taking with you the key points that I have emphasised throughout this book.

Keep reminding yourself, 'I am an amazing parent, and I am not alone!'

Glossary

Terms you may hear used to describe children with ADHD and related conditions:

Attention deficit disorder (ADD): The term commonly used to describe symptoms of inattention, distractibility, and poor working memory. Typically, those people with the above symptoms but without the hyperactivity of ADHD.[32]

---

32 A Russo, 'ADD vs ADHD symptoms: What's the difference? *ADDitude: Inside the ADHD Mind* (4 September 2019), www.additudemag.com/add-adhd-symptoms-difference, accessed 19 April 2021

Attention deficit hyperactivity disorder: ADHD is a developmental impairment of the brain's self-management system, its executive function.[33]

Autistic spectrum disorder (ASD): This is a complex neurobiological disorder that is characterised by difficulty communicating verbally and relating socially to others, alongside a need to engage in repetitive behaviours or language. Some common early signs noted by parents are delayed speech, restricted interests, not responding when called by name, and avoiding eye contact.[34]

Developmental delay or 'global development delay': A term used when a child takes longer to reach certain development milestones than other children.

Disability Living Allowance (DLA): An allowance that may help with the extra costs of looking after a child, paid to parents by the UK Government.[35]

Dyslexia: A learning disorder that involves difficulty reading due to problems identifying speech sounds and learning how they relate to letters and words. Also called reading disability, dyslexia affects areas of

---

33 T Brown, 'What is ADHD? Definition, myths and truth', *ADDitude: Inside the ADHD Mind* (no date), https://www.additudemag.com/adhd-definition, accessed 19 April 2021

34 J Rodden, 'What is autism spectrum disorder', *ADDitude: Inside the ADHD Mind* (no date), www.additudemag.com/what-is-autism-spectrum-disorder-asd, accessed 19 April 2021

35 Gov.UK, 'Disability Living Allowance (DLA) for children', www.gov.uk/disability-living-allowance-children, accessed 19 April 2021

the brain that process language and are responsible for learning to read.[36]

Dyspraxia – or developmental co-ordination disorder (DCD): A condition affecting physical co-ordination. It causes a child to perform less well than expected in daily activities for their age. They can appear to move awkwardly and/or be labelled as clumsy.[37]

Education Health and Care Plan (EHCP): An education, health and care (EHC) plan for children and young people aged up to twenty-five in England who need more support than is available through special educational needs support.[38]

Individualised Education Plan (IEP): This is a plan that outlines how teachers can plan for a child's individual progress. A SENCo can create one of these for your child and you can request this without needing to contact the local authority. You can request an IEP without a diagnosis and without having an EHCP.[39]

---

36 Mayo Clinic, 'Dyslexia', www.mayoclinic.org/diseases-conditions/dyslexia/symptoms-causes/syc-20353552, accessed 21 April 2021

37 NHS, 'Developmental co-ordination disorder (dyspraxia) in children', www.nhs.uk/conditions/developmental-coordination-disorder-dyspraxia, accessed 21 April 2021

38 Gov.UK, 'Children with special educational needs and disabilities (SEND)', www.gov.uk/children-with-special-educational-needs/extra-SEN-help, accessed 21 April 2021

39 National Austic Society, https://www.autism.org.uk/advice-and-guidance/topics/education/extra-help-at-school, accessed 19 April 2021

Neurodiverse: Not neurotypical (see below).

Neurotypical (NT): A term widely used to describe someone of typical development and with typical cognitive abilities.[40]

Obsessive compulsive disorder (OCD): A mental health disorder characterised by obsessions (recurring, unwanted thoughts) that lead to compulsions (repetitive behaviours or mental acts that an individual feels compelled to perform to 'undo' the obsession).[41]

Oppositional defiant disorder (ODD): This is a childhood behaviour disorder defined by a persistent pattern of hostile, vindictive, and defiant behaviour towards authority figures. Children with ODD are frequently irritable, argumentative, and disobedient. ODD may be diagnosed if this behaviour lasts for six months or longer.[42]

Special Education Needs Coordinator (SENCo): The person whose responsibility it is in a mainstream

---

40 Chaunie Brusie, 'All about recognizing a neurotypical', *Healthline* (14 July 2017) www.healthline.com/health/neurotypical, accessed 19 April 2021

41 Devon Frye, 'What is OCD? Obsessive compulsive disorder explained', www.additudemag.com/what-is-ocd-obsessive-compulsive-disorder, accessed 19 April 2021

42 Roberto Olivardia, 'What is oppositional defiant disorder (ODD)?', *ADDitude: Inside the ADHD Mind* (no date), www.additudemag.com/what-is-oppositional-defiant-disorder, accessed 19 april 2021

school to arrange extra help for those who need it.[43] They are usually teachers at the school. Most children with special educational needs will go to mainstream schools, and the law gives parents the right to say that they prefer this option for their child.[44]

43 https://contact.org.uk/help-for-families/information-advice-services/education-learning/introduction-to-special-educational-needs-in-england, accessed 19 April 2021
44 D Silas, 'The right to mainstream education', *senmagazine* (18 April 2020), https://senmagazine.co.uk/content/support-advice/law/10672/the-right-to-mainstream-education, accessed 30 April 2021

Appendix

Celebrities with ADHD and other conditions[45]

It is always helpful to know you are not alone. That doesn't just go for parents/carers, but for your child with ADHD, too. They might be interested to know that some of their heroes have the same or similar conditions and are successful in their chosen fields; these are just a few examples of celebrities with a diagnosis:

Cammi Granato, captain of the US Women's Ice Hockey team – ADHD

---

45 Adult Attention Deficit Disorder Center of Maryland, 'Famous people with ADHD', https://addadult.com/add-education-center/famous-people-with-adhd; Additude Editors, 'Famous people with ADHD', (22 March 2021), *ADDitude,* www.additudemag.com/slideshows/famous-people-with-adhd, accessed 19 April 2021

David Blaine, American magician and illusionist – ADHD

Emma Watson, award winning actress – ADHD

Heston Blumenthal, award winning and three Michelin star chef – ADHD[46]

Howie Mandel, comedian, America's Got Talent host – OCD and ADHD

Jim Carrey, American comedian, actor and producer, four-time Golden Globe Award nominee and two-time winner – ADHD

Justin Timberlake, award winning popstar and actor – OCD and ADHD

Louis Smith, British gymnast who won a silver medal at the London 2012 Olympics – ADHD

Michael Phelps, Olympic champion swimmer – ADHD

---

46   Adi Bloom, 'Heston Blumenthal: I have ADHD. But I wouldn't change it for the world', *TES* (21 December 2016), www.tes.com/news/heston-blumenthal-i-have-adhd-i-wouldnt-change-it-world

Michele Carter, Olympic Gold medal winner in shotput – ADHD and dyslexia[47]

Paris Hilton, hotel heiress, business woman and socialite – ADHD

Ryan Gosling, actor – ADHD

Simone Biles, American gymnast with four gold medals – ADHD

Sir Richard Branson, English business magnate and investor, founder of the Virgin Group – ADHD

Woody Harrelson, actor – ADHD and dyslexia

---

47 The Understood Team, 'Video: Michelle Carter wins Olympic Gold with dyslexia and ADHD', Understood (no date), www.understood. org/en/learning-thinking-differences/personal-stories/famous-people/video-michelle-carter-wins-olympic-gold-with-dyslexia-and-adhd, accessed 19 April 2021

Resources

Books

Bertin, Dr M, *Mindful Parenting for ADHD: A guide to cultivating calm, reducing stress and helping children thrive* (New Harbinger, 2015)

Green, Dr C and Chee, Dr K, *Understanding ADHD: A parent's guide to Attention Deficit Hyperactivity Disorder in children* (Ebury Digital, 2011)

Halligan, E, *My Child's Different: The lessons learned from one family's struggle to unlock their son's potential* (Crown House Publishing, 2018)

Hallowell, N and Ratey, Dr J, *Driven To Distraction: Recognizing and coping with attention deficit disorder* (Touchstone, 1995)

Kutscher, Dr ML, *ADHD: Living without brakes* (Jessica Kingsley, 2008)

Maguire, C, *Why Will No One Play With Me? The play better plan to help kids make friends and thrive* (Vermilion, 2019)

Saline, Dr S, *The ADHD Solution Deck: Strategies to help kids learn, reduce stress and improve family connections* (PESI Publishing and Media, 2020)

Saline, Dr S, *What Your ADHD Child Wishes You Knew: Working together to empower kids for success in school and life* (Tarcherperigee, 2018)

Online

ADHD Foundation
www.adhdfoundation.org.uk

ADHD (Help Guide)
www.helpguide.org/articles/add-adhd/when-your-child-has-attention-deficit-disorder-adhd.htm

ADHD Profile template
https://activepersonaldevelopment.co.uk/adhd-support-handbook-resources (see the Introduction for the password).

Adventures in Wisdom (Life coaching for kids)
https://adventuresinwisdom.com

Autism (Help Guide)
www.helpguide.org/articles/autism-learning-disabilities/helping-your-child-with-autism-thrive.htm

Autism Links
www.autismlinks.co.uk/support-groups

Children and Adults with Attention-Deficit/Hyperactivity Disorder (CHADD)
https://chadd.org/about-adhd/overview

Child and Adolescent Mental Health Services (CAMHS)
www.nhs.uk/mentalhealthservices

Child Mind Institute
www.childmind.org

The Coaching Academy
www.the-coaching-academy.com

Contact (For Families with Disabled Children)
www.contact.org.uk

Dr Sharon Saline, ADHD expert
www.drsharonsaline.com

Dyslexia (Mayo Clinic)
www.mayoclinic.org/diseases-conditions/dyslexia/
symptoms-causes/syc-20353552

Dyspraxia Foundation
www.dyspraxiafoundation.org.uk

Dyspraxia (NHS)
www.nhs.uk/conditions/
developmental-coordination-disorder-dyspraxia/
symptoms

EHCP Journeys
https://ehcpjourneys.com

Emotional Freedom Technique (The Tapping Solution)
www.thetappingsolution.com

The Habits Guide: How to Build Good Habits and
Break Bad Ones
www.jamesclear.com/habits

Impact Parents (Helping Parents Help Kids)
www.impactparents.com

Independent Provider of Special Education Advice
(IPSEA)
www.ipsea.org.uk

Learning disabilities and disorders (Help Guide)
www.helpguide.org/articles/autism-learning-
disabilities/learning-disabilities-and-disorders.htm

Meditation 101
www.gaiam.com/blogs/discover/meditation-
101-techniques-benefits-and-a-beginner-s-how-to

The National Attention Deficit Disorder Information
and Support Service (ADDISS)
www.addiss.co.uk

National Institute of Mental Health
www.nimh.nih.gov/statistics/1ANYANX_child.
shtml

Oppositional defiant disorder (ODD) (Mayo Clinic)
www.mayoclinic.org/diseases-conditions/
oppositional-defiant-disorder/symptoms-causes/syc-
20375831

VIA Character Strength Survey
www.viacharacter.org

Witherslack Group, provider of schools and
children's homes for children with special needs
www.witherslackgroup.co.uk

Young Minds Parents Helpline
https://youngminds.org.uk

A note from Jean

There's a great poem written by Andrea Chesterman-Smith. You can find it here:

www.cabinet.leicester.gov.uk:8071/documents/s114612/ADHD%20poem_.pdf

It describes many things about a child with ADHD that almost every parent of a child with ADHD can relate to. It's funny, thought-provoking, educating and inspiring. I urge you to read it, print it out, put it up somewhere you can see it on days when you're feeling low. It's a great pick-me-up.

You can also find other helpful resources at https://activepersonaldevelopment.co.uk/adhd-support-handbook-resources (see the Introduction for the password).

Acknowledgements

The first person I would like to acknowledge is my daughter, Lynnette. Our journey together learning about ADHD has made so many things clearer for us both. I thank her for finding the courage to share her challenges and allowing me to support her journey. Second, is my grandson, Mekhi, a beautiful and loving little boy. He awakened in me a passion for helping other children and families going through a similar journey. He is a real superhero! To Gavin, Kelly and Kyle, my other children, I am grateful and proud beyond words to have such cheerleaders in my corner. To all of my grandchildren you make me proud beyond words.

To Frank, my husband, my soulmate and the ultimate supporter. Thank you, darling, for walking this journey with me.

I feel very lucky to have a large extended family. My siblings, uncles, aunts, nieces, nephews, cousins and in-laws. Their love and support is always appreciated.

Special thanks also to my friends in Saint Vincent and The Grenadines – Geva and Tony Maskell, Cecelia and Wendell Brown, Joanne (who has now sadly passed), Denise and Junior – who I lived with during the writing process. They were generous enough to give me space, support and liquid pleasure to keep me going and I was lucky to enjoy such beautiful surroundings and friends who inspired me to share my story so far.

My mindset coach, Philippa Aldridge, encouraged me to follow my passion and has been so supportive of my desire to help others. Her continued support even when I did not want to shout about what I was doing was heartfelt and is much appreciated.

My fellow coach and friend, Kandy Holgate, a courageous and beautiful spirit, inspired and encouraged me during the writing process. Thank you, I am forever grateful for our friendship.

Having people read my manuscript to ensure it would be of value and resonate with those it is aimed at was critical for me to know that I was on the right track.

Claire Baker, Debbie Nori, Lindsey Carr and Lorraine Thomas all helped me refine the content and focus. Without their feedback and support, I may not have been able to complete this book. They all supported and encouraged me to continue. Thank you all for your time, energy and encouragement.

During this last year I have worked with a group of coaches, consultants and fellow entrepreneurs as part of an enlightenment programme. Eileen McCotter Davies, a talented holistic mindset coach, has helped me to reveal my truth and to get out of my own way in terms of moving my life and business forward. Members of our group have been encouraging and inspirational in supporting my growth. Thank you all, and in particular to Tony, Andy, Gilly, Georgia, Tracy and Phillipa.

Thank you also to my accountant, Alison Harrison and the team at Harmonea, for your continued support and encouragement.

Many of my entrepreneurial friends in business have watched and encouraged my growth. Jo Beardsmore-Dilks, Cerys Keneally, Vassia Sarri, Karen Burge, Karen Kimberly and Mina Leal-Birch, my bookkeeper to name a few. Thank you all for your continued support and friendship.

Thank you also to my personal assistant, Helen Cook, for all your encouragement and support.

My friends in faith are important to me and have always supported my efforts by providing spiritual guidance, encouragement and space to be me. In particular, Donna Wade, Pam Patterson and Annick McKenzie have provided a support system through tough times and happier times, which I will be forever grateful for.

To the wonderful people who permitted me to share their personal story in this book in order to help others.

A special thanks to Lucy McCarraher, my book coach, for encouraging and believing in me and helping me to make this possible. To everyone involved in producing it at Rethink Press.

Finally, my mum and dad, who I know would have loved to have been a part of this journey, who were always supportive and encouraged me to follow my dreams. I know Dad would say, 'Stand tall and be proud, Jean.'

The Author

Jean Gibson Assoc CIPD (Chartered Institute of Personnel Development), Diploma in personal performance coaching, certified WISDOM Coach® and Accredited Flow Consultant.

With a caring and understated nature, a long career in the airline industry and an entrepreneurial flair, Jean has spent over thirty-five years working in IT and learning and development. She has managed hundreds of staff in their career development and been involved in delivering and supporting IT projects across the UK and worldwide. She is recognised for her achievements in workplace diversity. Alongside full-time work, she also ran a part-time business as a CV writer and career consultant for over ten years.

Jean has transitioned from corporate life to running her own business as a qualified personal performance coach, certified WISDOM Coach® and accredited Talent Dynamics Flow Consultant, working to improve the lives of children, parents and professionals through coaching. Her passion is helping children with learning or behavioural challenges develop a positive mindset and the skills to deal with the ups and downs of life; and supporting young people and adults to become the best version of themselves and fulfil their potential. Her work includes helping children and young people with neurodevelopmental conditions, such as autism spectrum disorder and ADHD, as well as children who display challenging behaviour, lack self-confidence and low self-esteem, and who suffer with anxiety and stress-related symptoms.

In her personal time, Jean has volunteered as a school governor, supported a Saturday school, run a networking group for small businesses, become an enterprise advisor and was active in her community as a parish councillor. She has established support groups, both online and in person, and has a passion for helping others.

THE AUTHOR

Jean's oldest daughter was diagnosed with dyslexia when she was at school, at a time when there was limited information and support available. Later, her grandson was diagnosed with ADHD, dyspraxia and global developmental delay, with a younger brother and older sister also showing symptoms. Inspired by her family, Jean found the courage to share their story to provide insights, encouragement, tools and guidance to help you navigate your ADHD journey.

🌐 www.activepersonaldevelopment.co.uk

f Business page: www.facebook.com/activepersonaldevelopment.co.uk

f ADHD Revolution support group: www.facebook.com/groups/theadhdrevolution (online)

f ADHD Buckinghamshire parents support group: www.facebook.com/groups/2080065458963820 (in person)

in www.linkedin.com/in/jsrich4242

© https://www.instagram.com/jean_apd/

159

Printed in Great Britain
by Amazon

18088025R00098